# THE POEMS OF STEPHEN CRANE

## STEPHEN CRANE IN THE YEAR OF *THE BLACK RIDERS*

To Dr. A. L. Mitchell:

Hartwood, N.Y., January 29, 1896

My dear Doctor: I was in Virginia when your letter came to Hartwood and so did not get it until yesterday. You delight me with your appreciation and yet too it makes me afraid. I did not bend under the three hills of ridicule which were once upon my shoulders but I dont know that I am strong enough to withstand the kind things that are now sometimes said to me. I have a strong desire to sit down and look at myself. Always your friend

Stephen Crane

*From the original inscribed photograph in the Lilly Library of Indiana University.*

# THE POEMS OF
# STEPHEN CRANE

*A Critical Edition by*

JOSEPH KATZ

COOPER SQUARE PUBLISHERS, INC.
*New York* *1966*

Copyright © 1966 By Joseph Katz

Published By Cooper Square Publishers, Incorporated
59 Fourth Avenue, New York, New York 10003

Printed in the United States of America

Library of Congress Catalog Card No. 65-17181

*Design By Lynn Hatfield*

*FOR EDWIN H. CADY*
*AND HORST FRENZ*

## Acknowledgements

Two important debts are recorded on another page. I owe additional thanks to Edwin H. Cady for stimulating this work and for commenting on the stages through which it progressed. James K. Hastie patiently listened to my flights of theory and read through many manuscripts, Vincent Starrett commented on an early version, and Fredson Bowers on the editorial principles.

Librarians and libraries of considerable assistance to me were David A. Randall, Miss Geneva Warner, Mrs. Doris M. Read, and William Cagle of the Lilly and University Libraries of Indiana University; Roland Baughman and Kenneth A. Lohf of the Butler Library of Columbia University; William H. Runge, Miss Anne Freudenberg and Miss Elizabeth Ryall of the Alderman Library of the University of Virginia; John S. Mayfield and Lester G. Wells of the Syracuse University Library; Miss Anna Brooke Allan and James W. Patton of the University of North Carolina Library; John D. Gordan of the Berg Collection of the New York Public Library. I offer additional thanks to these institutions for permission to publish material of which they are the possessors.

I owe further debts to Clifton Waller Barrett; to Robert W. Stallman; to Owen Thomas; to William A. Koshland of Alfred A. Knopf Incorporated; to Gay Wilson Allen; to David H. Dickason; to Maurice Bassan; to Pierre Baillet; to Matthew J. Bruccoli; to Daniel G. Hoffman; and to Henry Chafetz and Sidney B. Solomon of Cooper Square Publishers.

For permission to publish from the manuscripts and letters of Stephen Crane, and for permission to reprint from *The Work of*

*Stephen Crane* and *The Collected Poems,* I thank Alfred A. Knopf Incorporated, owners of the literary rights to Crane's writings.

Finally, I thank Karen for the intelligence, the understanding, and the fairly consistent good humor with which she has borne her trials.

Joseph Katz

# Contents

# Contents

# Contents

UNCOLLECTED POEMS

*"LEGENDS"*

WAR IS KIND

xi

# Contents

# Contents

xiii

# Contents

# Illustrations

xv

# Introduction

"BLACK RIDERS CAME FROM THE SEA"

"Personally, I like my little book of poems, 'The Black Riders,' better than I do 'The Red Badge of Courage'," Stephen Crane said in mid-career. "The reason is, I suppose, that the former is the more ambitious effort. In it I aim to give my ideas of life as a whole, so far as I know it, and the latter is a mere episode, or rather an amplification."[1] Despite the apparent clash of this statement with the critical consensus, Crane's remark is largely ignored. For the influence that his poetry has had on the direction of modern American poetry, for the illumination that it brings to the development of a significant American author, and for the understanding that it contributes to the relationship between the American writer and the "new publishing" of the 'nineties, Crane's poetry is relatively unexplored.

The history of that poetry properly begins with Crane's first, premature, contact with the fringe-world of American letters. On 18 August 1891 the New York *Tribune* carried "Howells Discussed at Avon-by-the-Sea," a routine report of the doings at the Methodist resort on the New Jersey shore.[2] One of the

---

[1] Crane to John Northern Hilliard, [1897?], in R. W. Stallman and Lillian Gilkes, eds., *Stephen Crane: Letters* (New York, 1960), p. 159. Compare Crane to Hilliard, 2 January 1896, *Letters*, p. 95.

[2] Reprinted in Donald Pizer, "Crane Reports Garland on Howells," *Modern Language Notes*, LXX (January 1955), 37-39. The obscurities in

more interesting of the activities sponsored by the group was the School of Literature of the Seaside Assembly, actually a series of lectures on literature delivered by Hamlin Garland. Crane regularly covered the shore news as a representative of his brother Townley's press bureau, and the clipping of his article provided an introduction to Garland. Garland was pleasantly surprised by the accuracy of Crane's story and by their mutual interest in sports; Crane in turn was pleased by Garland's views, his appearance ("like a nice Jesus Christ" [3]), and—understandably—by the attentions of an established author. The two accompanied their conversations by throwing a baseball back and forth, and soon developed a pleasant, if casual, relationship.

They picked up the threads of their acquaintance the following August, and the baseball resumed its flight. This time Crane casually displayed a report of an Asbury Park mechanics' parade—an indiscreet presentation of a shabby line of laborers straggling past a review of nattily dressed, idle vacationers—and just as casually announced that the ensuing fuss resulted in his being let out of his job.[4] Garland deplored the situation, but Crane was, after all, no more than a talented young reporter and a casual acquaintance. Without the

the dating of the relationship between Crane and Hamlin Garland are dispelled by Pizer in "The Garland-Crane Relationship," *Huntington Library Quarterly*, XXIV (November 1960), 75-82, and by Olov W. Fryckstedt in "Crane's *Black Riders*: A Discussion of Dates," *Studia Neophilologica*, XXXIV (1962), 282-293. These collect much of the evidence for dating the creation of Crane's first group of poems.

[3] Thomas Beer, *Stephen Crane*: *A Study in American Letters* (New York, 1923), p. 60.

[4] Victor A. Elconin reprinted "On the New Jersey Coast" and discussed the controversy surrounding it in his "Stephen Crane at Asbury Park," *American Literature*, XX (November 1948), 275-289. See also John Berryman, *Stephen Crane* (New York, 1950), pp. 43-44, and R. W. Stallman, *Stephen Crane: An Omnibus* (New York, 1952), pp. 21-22.

amazing prescience in which he was so interested, Garland could have had little reason to believe that within a few years Crane would do much to further the revolution in literature for which he and William Dean Howells worked.

A portent of that possibility was the yellow-wrapped copy of *Maggie* the postman brought in March, 1893. Crane had been indiscreet again. It was an age of nickel and dime novels, and an era when Anthony Comstock and the Society for the Suppression of Vice were powerful, and the novelette was doomed: few would pay fifty cents for 160 pages of story by an unknown, and certainly not for the story of "a girl of the streets" who went undamned. Most copies Crane gave away; others he used to light his fire. Garland's copy was signed simply "The Author," but he had heard the rumors that Crane had planted, and he thought that he noted sufficient reasons in the style to confirm the ascription.

On the strength of the power of *Maggie,* Garland interested Howells in Crane. As part of his practice of aiding worthy unknowns without asking allegiance in return, Howells had assisted George Pellew, Ralph Keeler, Bret Harte, and Garland. Sometime between the twenty-ninth of March and the eighth of April, Howells had Crane to tea, praised him above Howells's good friend, "Mark Twain," and read to him from one of the posthumously-published volumes of Emily Dickinson's verse.[5] Howells was taken with Crane, "struck almost as

---

[5] The later comparison of Crane's verse with that of Dickinson makes the episode significant. Its source is John D. Barry's "A Note on Stephen Crane," *Bookman,* XIII (April 1901), 148, published before the comparison became commonplace. Corwin Knapp Linson, Crane's closest friend at the time, reported the meeting with Howells in *My Stephen Crane* (Syracuse, New York, 1958), p. 44, but did not mention the reading. Linson did note that he had not heard of the meeting from Crane. Since Howells thought much of Dickinson's verse, it is quite possible that he read to Crane from either *Poems by Emily Dickinson* (1890) or *Poems by Emily Dickinson: Second*

much by his presence as by his mind,"[6] while Crane shamelessly dropped Howells's name into many of his letters; and yet it is difficult to evaluate the relationship.

Quite possibly it was the effect of the poetry he had heard that night, probably it was that William Dean Howells had sufficiently admired that poetry to read it to his company, that stimulated Crane to try his hand at serious verse. He had undoubtedly written poetry of a sort before he composed the pieces for *The Black Riders,* and it is even possible that the legendary volume of erotic poems, *Cantharides,* stems from this period.[7] But the survival of "Ah, haggard purse, why ope thy mouth" *(118)* —which Linson, *My Stephen Crane,* pp. 13-14, sets in December, 1892—suggests that much of this pre-verse was little more than poetical doodling.[8] Internal and external evidence tend to support the generally accepted belief that *The Black Riders* was written soon after the meeting with Howells. From the style, the subject matter, and the coherent treatment of the poems, stems a conclusion that they were products of one intensive, continuous period of composition. And despite the confusion spread by Crane, the usually accurate Linson, *My Stephen Crane,* p. 48, recalled that it was in mid-February, 1894, that Crane appeared with his "lines."[9]

---

*Series* (1891). *Poems: Third Series* was not published until 1896, long after the meeting and Crane's composition of *The Black Riders.*

6 W. D. Howells to Cora Crane, 29 July 1900, in *Letters,* p. 306.

7 *"Cantharides*—Said to have been a collection of erotic verse, the manuscript of which was seen by several persons. Untraced." From Vincent Starrett's *Stephen Crane: A Bibliography* (Philadelphia, 1923), pp. 10-11. Efforts to trace this collection through Mr. Starrett and through the Institute for Sex Research, Indiana University, have proven fruitless.

8 See also Daniel G. Hoffman, *The Poetry of Stephen Crane* (New York, 1957), p. 181. Numbers in italic in this text refer to the List of Poems.

9 Thomas Beer, *Stephen Crane,* p. 119, declared, "A fog rests on the birth of 'Black Riders'...." The haze surrounding the dating of *The Black Riders* must be laid to Crane. To John Northern Hilliard, he wrote that "In my

I looked here
~~And~~ I looked there
No where could I see my love.
And —this time —
She was in my heart.
Truly then I have no complaint
For 'though she be fair and fairer
She is none so fair
As herself in my heart.

509 cat. 28 Jl 54

※ VIII In Black Riders. last lines "She is none so fair as she (as
In my heart " printed)

Draft B: "I looked here | I looked there" (8).
Facsimile of the manuscript in the Syracuse University Library.

Almost immediately, Crane left his billet on Twenty-third Street and journeyed to One Hundred and Fifth Street to attempt to recruit Garland's aid in finding a market for them.[10]

Garland's reports of this meeting have passed into the folklore of American literary history.[11] In the pocket of his ulster Crane carried the manuscripts of his poems. Garland, at first amused, gradually realized their power:

---

twenty-third year, I wrote *The Black Riders*" (*Letters*, p. 95) , while Beer (*Stephen Crane*, p. 119) recorded that at one time Crane had remarked, "I wrote the things in February of 1893," (when he was twenty-two years old) . The difference of a full year in the life of a man who died before he reached the age of thirty is quite significant.

Fortunately, Harvey Wickham, "Stephen Crane at College," *American Mercury*, VII (March 1926) , 291-97, may be safely disregarded: " 'A fog rests on the birth of "The Black Riders," says a recent authority. Maybe so. But I have good reasons for thinking that this first voice of free verse crying in the wilderness was reduced to words in three days at Twin Lakes [in Pike County, Pennsylvania, a region in which Crane and his friends camped in 1893-1894]. Crane subsequently told me that it was the outcome of a fit of desperation. 'No one would print a line of mine,' he said, 'and I just had to do something odd to attract attention.' " Not only had Wickham never been to Twin Lakes with Crane; his questionable statements about the origins of *George's Mother* serve to detract from his credibility.

10 Crane shared an apartment with Frederic Gordon (the artist who prepared the designs for the binding of *The Black Riders*) and a number of artists and illustrators in the old Art Students' League building at 143 East Twenty-third Street. The close association with artists—Linson, for example, was a noted illustrator who painted the well-known portrait of Crane that is now in the Alderman Library—has made the influence of painting and the pictorial on his writing a legitimate field of inquiry.

11 Garland wrote divergent accounts of that meeting: "Stephen Crane: A Soldier of Fortune," *Saturday Evening Post*, CLXXIII (28 July 1900) , 16-17, and *Book-Lover*, II (Autumn 1900) , 6-7; "Stephen Crane as I Knew Him," *Yale Review*, III (April 1914) , 494-506; "Roadside Meetings of a Literary Nomad," *Bookman*, LXX (January 1930) , 523-28; *Roadside Meetings* (New York, 1930) , pp. 189-206. In these reports, Garland's interest in Crane as an exemplar of the automatic writer responding to the influence of occult forces became the overpowering shaping principle. Pizer's "The Garland-Crane Relationship" reconciles these accounts convincingly.

They were at once quaintly humorous and audacious, unrhymed and almost without rhythm, but the figures employed with masterly brevity were colossal. They suggested some of the French translations of Japanese verses, at other times they carried the sting and compression of Emily Dickinson's verse and the savage philosophy of Olive Shriner [sic], and yet they were not imitative.[12]

Were there more? "I have four of five up here all in a little row," Crane replied, and—without a moment's hesitation—dashed off "God fashioned the ship of the world carefully" (6). Consciously or not, Crane had struck just that attitude that would assure Garland's rapt interest. The future president of the American Psychical Association, Garland had just returned from a series of sittings with a psychic, had collaborated on an article describing the psychic phenomena he had witnessed, and was at least abnormally sensitive to the presence of unworldly forces.[13] Perhaps it was Crane's discomfort with

---

[12] Garland, *Roadside Meetings*, pp. 193-94. A wave of interest in Japanese culture swept over France following Perry's opening of Japan to trade with the West in 1854. The influence appeared not only in verse, but in painting, music, and dress. Olive Schreiner (1855-1920) was a South African writer and crusader for women's rights who, in the last two decades of the nineteenth century, won popularity under the name of "Ralph Iron." Crane expressed admiration for her *The Story of an African Farm* (See Linson, *My Stephen Crane*, p. 34) and undoubtedly read *Dreams*, an allegorical cycle. Her influence on Crane's poetry has been explored by Carlin T. Kindilien, "Stephen Crane and the 'Savage Philosophy' of Olive Schreiner," *Boston University Studies in English*, III (Summer 1957), 97-107, and by Hoffman, *The Poetry of Stephen Crane*, pp. 195-200. The influence is probably more a confluence since the dream-allegory, a direct descendant of the parable, flooded the literary market throughout the nineteenth century; and since Crane, son of a minister and the product of a line of prominent Methodist clergymen, would have been weaned on the parent form, the parable.

[13] Hamlin Garland, T. E. Allen, and B. O. Flower, "Report of Dark Seances, with a Non-Professional Psychic, for Voices and the Movement of Objects without Contact," *Psychical Review*, II (November 1893-February 1894), 152-77.

the nonsense that traditionally surrounds the literary man that prevented him from disabusing Garland,[14] but Garland's belief moved him enthusiastically to show the poems he had seen to Howells.

While Howells agreed that the poems were the output of a singularly creative mind, despite their resemblances to the works of others, he did have reservations.[15] After one venture in which he failed to interest Henry Mills Alden in publishing Crane's lines in *Harper's Magazine,* Howells wrote Crane that "I wish you had given them more form, for then things so striking would have found a public ready made for them; as it is they will have to make one."[16] And eight months later he confessed that the poems were "too orphic," not "solid and real," and he predicted the demise of the "'prose-poem'."[17] Howells believed that Crane's apparent lack of form implied a break with poetic tradition, a break so great as to interfere with complete communication; this complaint underlay Howells's later review of *The Black Riders.*[18] In any case, neither Howells nor Garland found the publisher for Crane's book of poetry; that task fell to John D. Barry, editor of the *Forum* and friend and publisher of Hamlin Garland.

"Shortly before I left for the West," wrote Garland, "he [Crane] called to tell me that he had shown his verses to Mr.

---

[14] For example, Crane steadily refused to call his productions "poems," but insisted on labelling them "pills" or "lines." Thus the significance of the titles, *The Black Riders and Other Lines* and "Lines by Stephen Crane." To Nellie Crouse he stressed the point: "I am sorry that you did not find the 'two poems'—mind you, I never call them poems myself—in the *Philistine.*" See *Letters,* p. 96.

[15] Garland recorded Howells's judgment in "Stephen Crane: A Soldier of Fortune," reprinted in *Letters,* p. 303.

[16] Howells to Crane, 18 March 1894, *Letters,* p. 31.

[17] Howells to Crane, 2 October 1894, *Letters,* p. 40.

[18] "Life and Letters," *Harper's Weekly,* XL (25 January 1896), 79.

John D. Barry and that Mr. Barry had 'fired them off to Cope-
land and Day.' "[19] In a very real sense, Crane did find "a public
ready made" for his verse, a public that felt the impact of Wil-
liam Morris on American publishing. Morris reacted violently
against the ugliness that resulted from the mechanical revolu-
tion in England, turning to the Middle Ages for the period of
art's fullest development.[20] In the hands of the scribe, for exam-
ple, the medieval book became a thing of beauty, to be looked at
as well as into, and Morris saw no reason why a mass-produced
volume could not meet the same standard. If, in designing his
Kelmscott Press books, he erred perhaps too much on the side
of beauty (to echo Holbrook Jackson for a moment[21])—pro-
ducing books so covered with ornament and intricate
"Gothic" type faces that they were difficult to read, books
bound in vellum that would not stay open, books so heavy
that a lectern was a necessity, and books so expensive that only
a few could buy—it was no great matter; he had indicated an
aesthetic in publishing, and his followers frequently realized
the possibilities he had revealed.

In this country the trend took two directions, and Crane was
involved in both. Men such as Elbert Hubbard applied

---

[19] Garland, *Roadside Meetings*, p. 200. Barry (1866-1942) was so taken with
Crane, so impressed by his achievement, that he introduced Crane's verse to
the public through a reading (after Crane shyly declined a personal ap-
pearance) before the Uncut Leaves Society at Sherry's on 14 April 1894.
Among those who attended was the wife of the noted critic and poet, Edmund
Clarence Stedman. Stedman later included some of Crane's poetry in his im-
portant *American Anthology* (1900), Publication 27. The reading at Sherry's
was reported in the New York *Tribune* of 16 April 1894 (reprinted in Linson,
*My Stephen Crane*, pp. 55-56).

[20] *William Morris: Prose, Verse, Lectures, and Essays*, G. D. H. Cole, ed.
(London, 1948), p. 476.

[21] Holbrook Jackson, "The Typography of William Morris," in his *The
Printing of Books* (London, 1938), and reprinted in Paul A. Bennett, ed.,
*Books and Printing* (Cleveland and New York, 1963), pp. 233-38.

Morris's doctrine with little sensitivity and produced artsy-craftsy books compounded of fine materials, indifferent workmanship, and bad taste. But men such as Herbert Copeland and Frederick Holland Day helped to stimulate the production of books that were at once experimental and tasteful.[22]

Small and light, they are real reading volumes, favorably distinguished in their charming bindings from the drab mechanical carelessness of the ordinary editions of those years. Here, too, one finds the use of color and ornament, gold or silver stamped upon simple cloth covers, or boards completely covered with paper, gray or in colorful ornamental patterns.[23]

In its six years of existence (1893-1899), the house reflected the wealth, eccentricity, and artistic staunchness of Frederick Day, and the knowledgeability and restraint of Herbert Copeland. Of the ninety-six titles in the catalog, fifty-four were books of poetry. The inclusion of Stephen Crane's *The Black Riders and Other Lines* among these can be set down in part to the friendship between Copeland and John D. Barry during their days at Harvard, at a time when that institution turned out many of the leaders of the experimental movement in publishing.[24]

But while refusal to compromise marked the firm of Copeland and Day, it was also a characteristic of their new author. On 9 September 1894, Crane responded to a suggestion that certain poems would best be omitted from the volume with a frosty refusal:

---

[22] A useful sketch of the principles, practices, and fortunes of Copeland and Day is Joe Walker Kraus, "Messrs. Copeland & Day—Publishers to the 1890's," *Publishers' Weekly*, CXLI (21 March 1942), 1168-1171.

[23] Hellmut Lehmann-Haupt, *The Book in America* (New York, 1951), p. 324.

[24] Barry attended Harvard from 1884-1889, Copeland from 1887-1891.

xxvi

It seems to me that you cut all the ethical sense out of the book. All the anarchy, perhaps. It is the anarchy which I particularly insist upon. From the poems which you keep you could produce what might be termed a "nice little volume of verse by Stephen Crane," but for me there would be no satisfaction. The ones which refer to God, I believe you condemn altogether. I am obliged to have them in when my book is printed.[25]

Unfortunately, as an almost complete unknown, Crane was in a poor position to be uncompromising. It is conceivable that either Crane or his publishers asked Howells to mediate the dispute, for the letter in which Howells predicts the demise of the "prose-poem" might be read as a gentle suggestion that Crane come to his senses. But it is not really necessary to posit any such intervention, for while Crane could insist on his way, he was realist enough to know when he must submit. At any rate, Copeland and Day followed with a letter detailing the omissions they would insist upon. Their note has about it an air of finality:

Dear Sir:

We hope you will pardon this delay regarding your verses now with us, and beg to say that we will be glad to publish them if you will agree to omitting those beginning as follows.

1.     A god it is said
       Marked a sparrow's fall

2.[d]   To the maiden
       The sea was a laughing meadow

3.[d]   A god came to a man
       And spoke in this wise.

---

[25] Crane to Copeland and Day, 9 September 1894, *Letters,* pp. 39-40.

4.th     There was a man with a tongue of wood.

5.th     The traveller paused in kindness

6.th     Should you stuff me with flowers

7.th     One came from the skies.


Should you still object to omitting so many we will rest content to print all but the first three in the above list, though all of them appear to us as *far* better left unprinted.

We are sending by post a couple of drawings either of which might please you to be used by way of fronticepiece for the book; one would be something illustrative, while the other would be symbolic in a wide sense.

As to a title for the book, the one you suggest is acceptable if nothing better occurs to you. The omission of titles for separate poems is an idea we most heartily agree with.

We are also sending a blank form to receive your signature should you decide to entrust the book to our hands: a duplicate will be sent to you upon the return of this copy.

Kindly let us hear from you at as early a date as possible.[26]


Crane's reply on 30 October is evidently a curt note of capitulation enclosing the title poem—"Black riders came from the sea" (*1*) —and notifying them of a change of address.[27]

---

[26] Copeland and Day to Crane, 19 October 1894. The letter is in an unidentified holograph, on a sheet formed by folding Copeland and Day's letterhead in half. The script covers verso 1 and continues on recto 2. It is through the permission of Clifton Waller Barrett and the Alderman Library, University of Virginia, that this important letter is first published.

[27] *Letters*, p. 40. During this period in his life Crane changed his address often. In April and May, for example, the return address varied from 111

None of the poems listed by Copeland and Day appears in *The Black Riders,* and apparently only four of the seven survive. "To the maiden | The sea was blue meadow" *(78)* and "There was a man with tongue of wood" *(91)* were included in the second collection of Crane's poetry, *War Is Kind;* but while Cora Crane attempted to have "A god came to a man | And said to him thus" *(120)* and "One came from the skies" *(119)* published after Stephen's death, they were not printed until 1957, in Hoffman's *The Poetry of Stephen Crane.*[28]

The four surviving poems appear to support Crane's complaint that his publishers wished to "cut all the ethical sense out of the book." While the title, *The Black Riders and Other Lines,* suggests that the volume is little more than a miscellany, it is actually more cohesive than that. Crane had apparently anticipated his comment to John Northern Hilliard on his purpose in the volume in a letter to *Leslie's Weekly:* "My aim was to comprehend in it [*The Black Riders*] the thoughts I have had about life in general . . . ."[29]

These thoughts about life in general are placed within an

---

West Thirty-third Street, to Camp Interlaken, Pennsylvania, to his brother William's house at Hartwood, Sullivan County, New York, and back to 143 East Twenty-third Street. It was poverty as much as whim that caused the frequent moves, but this established the nomadic pattern of Crane's life. Fortunately, since Crane rarely carried a consistent source of supply of paper with him, it is frequently possible to date a manuscript of the poetry by means of the type of paper on which it was written.

[28] Joseph Katz, "Cora Crane and the Poetry of Stephen Crane," *Papers of the Bibliographical Society of America,* LVII (Fourth Quarter, 1964) , 469-476. Consult Publication 34 in the Materials Collated section of the Bibliographies for a list of the poems first printed in Hoffman's book. Since *The Poetry of Stephen Crane* is a most important critical work that attempts also to provide the texts of previously unavailable poems, poems first printed there are collated in this edition.

[29] Crane to an editor of *Leslie's Weekly,* ["About November, 1895"], *Letters,* p. 79.

envelope: "Black riders came from the sea" (*1*) carries with it
the suggestion of the Apocalypse (Revelations 6.2, 4, 5, 8)
and the rider carrying the balances, serving as a kind of Invo-
cation to the muse of truth; while "A spirit sped | Through
spaces of night" (*68*) closes the volume with the ironic com-
ment that God allows the soothsayer to speak truth—the "Sin"
of the first poem—then, having tricked him into blasphemy,
strikes him dead. Between the envelope, a persona provides a
coherent, if young, view of life. In the parable-like poems,
there is the exposure of the absurdity of life; in the lyrics, the
implication that despite its absurdities life is worthwhile,
brightened by a love that is no less significant for the despair
at the sham in which it must exist and which must crush it.
Daniel G. Hoffman has provided, in *The Poetry of Stephen
Crane*, a convincing survey of many of the themes central to
Crane's poetry; these are the bases of Crane's aesthetic.

The four poems that survive of those that Copeland and
Day wished to omit from *The Black Riders* indicate the path
of "the ride of Sin." "A god came to a man" is a version of the
temptation of Adam in which the deity confronts man directly.
Adam responds with the standard refutation of the doctrine
of predestination, an argument of which Crane's Methodist
forebears would have entirely approved: God has created
man with his appetites and his weaknesses; if man could
surmount these limitations, he would become greater than God.
Actually, as the tone of "Adam's" response suggests, the power
of constructing such an argument places man above God. In
"One came from the skies," Christ's divinity is slighted by the
addition of "—They said—" (the lining is significant here, as
it is in all of Crane's poems) , and the sacrament of marriage
is repudiated. The man sees the band that ties him to the
woman as a band of gold, while the woman and a second man
—an interloper—see it as iron. The second man leaves without

acting on his conviction that the marriage bond is worthless, and in that he is at fault: the iron shackle has fettered him. Some time later, Crane must have realized the impossibility of publishing the poem in its original form, and penciled out the last three lines of the poem: "For shackles fit apes. | He is not brave | Who leaves the iron on doves." Cora Crane—who was probably not legally married to Crane and who was evidently merely separated from her husband while she was living with Crane—accepted the deletion in her compilation of Stephen's poems.

In the context of *The Black Riders*, the remaining two omitted poems also would have taken on connotations of blasphemy. "To the maiden," in addition to being a "point of view" poem of the kind for which Thomas Wentworth Higginson praised Crane,[30] succeeds in opposing the shallow romanticism of the maiden with a view of the capricious malignancy of Nature that anticipated Crane's later stress on the utter indifference of the universe to the fate of the individual (an attitude that was reinforced by Crane's experience in the open boat). And "There was a man with tongue of wood," while self-mocking, certainly could be interpreted in context as the defiant dedication of an iconoclastic book to the Supreme Ikon. To Copeland and Day these may have been the most sinful (certainly "There was a man with tongue of wood," in the version that they saw, sinned against the ears of the late nineteenth century), but their omission did not change the character of the book. Undoubtedly, Crane's hasty addition of "Black riders came from the sea," submitted after his capitulation, assured that.

---

[30] [Thomas Wentworth Higginson], "Recent Poetry," *The Nation,* LXI (24 October 1896) , 296. Ascription has been made on the basis of the published index to the *Nation.*

Nevertheless, the contract was signed and the details of publication were arranged. Crane had decided on the title of the book and had suggested that the poems be printed without individual titles (a practice he later reaffirmed in his periodical publications of the poetry, although he frequently referred to the poems by title in his letters and in his private notes), and—after rejecting Copeland and Day's suggestion that "old English" type be used—he agreed on simple, "roman" capital letters to be used throughout, the poems to be printed one to a page and to be identified by numerals.[31] This peculiarity of presentation became one of Crane's trademarks as a poet, proving to be the most obvious trait to critics and reviewers who were unable or unwilling to proceed further. In a last-minute flurry, he arranged for Frederic C. Gordon to submit a floral motif for the binding and for the volume to be dedicated to Hamlin Garland. About seven months after the contract was signed, *The Black Riders and Other Lines* appeared. Stephen Crane had at last published a book for which he would receive royalties. He was an author and a poet, and he awaited word of his reception.

---

[31] See Copeland and Day to Crane, 19 October 1894, p. 17 above, for their assent to the omission of individual titles, and Crane to Copeland and Day, 10 December 1894, *Letters,* p. 42, for his remark that "I have grown somewhat frightened at the idea of old English type since some of my recent encounters with it have made me think I was working out a puzzle."

II "A NEWSPAPER IS A COLLECTION OF HALF-INJUSTICES"

The publication of *The Black Riders and Other Lines* made little immediate difference to anyone but Stephen Crane and his supporters. It would be a distortion to say with Thomas Beer that "the reading nation was told at once that Stephen Crane was mad," but it would be equally wrong to agree with Thomas F. O'Donnell's suggestion that Crane's reception was enthusiastic.[32] Actually, the reading nation heard very little "at once" of *The Black Riders*. The first comments came from those in the Howells-Garland-Barry camp and from their opponents; as with other first books of verse, *The Black Riders* attracted attention initially for its associations and later for its achievements. When the phenomenal sales of *The Red Badge of Courage* brought forth Crane as the center of two public controversies, the poetry became of wider interest and was frequently reviewed in the context of the popularity of the novel.[33] But if the early com-

---

[32] Beer, *Stephen Crane*, p. 120; O'Donnell, "A Note on the Reception of Crane's *The Black Riders*," *American Literature*, XXIV (May 1952), 233-235.

Reviews of *The Black Riders* additional to those cited in this section are "Stephen Crane: Author of 'The Black Riders and Other Lines'," *Bookman*, I (May 1895), 229-230; "Literary Notes," New York *Daily Tribune*, 9 June 1895, p. 24; "New Volumes of Verse," *Book Buyer*, XII, 5 (June 1895), 298; *Munsey's Magazine*, XII, 4 (July 1895), 430; Rupert Hughes, "The Rise of Stephen Crane," *Godey's Magazine*, CXXXIII (September 1896), 316-319; Thomas Wentworth Higginson, "Recent Poetry," *Nation*, LXI (24 October 1896), 296; M. A. DeWolfe Howe, Jr., "Six Books of Verse," *Atlantic Monthly*, LXXVII (February 1896), 271-272; William Dean Howells, "Life and Letters," *Harper's Weekly*, XL (25 January 1896), 79. Half of these reviews were occasioned by the success of *The Red Badge*.

[33] Civil War veterans insisted that the author of *The Red Badge* had to have had actual battle experience in the War, while chauvinists argued against the claim that it was the English who had first discovered the book. Less

ments are only minimally significant as an index of the reception of *The Black Riders,* they are of major importance in their influence on the ways in which Crane's poems were later discussed.

For example, the strange format of the book combined with the unusual qualities of the poems to suggest that *The Black Riders* resulted from an intentionally eccentric posture of the poet. What actually was the mordant expression of Crane's dissatisfaction with the religious traditions of his family, appeared to many to be related to the characteristics of Oscar Wilde, Aubrey Beardsley, and the decadents. "Mr. Stephen Crane is the Aubrey Beardsley of poetry." began the friendly review in the influential *Bookman.*[34]

When one first takes up his little book of verse and notes the quite too Beardsleyesque splash of black upon its staring white boards, and then on opening it discovers that the "lines" are printed wholly in capitals, and that they are unrhymed and destitute of what most poets regard as rhythm, the general impression is of a writer who is bidding for renown wholly on the basis of his eccentricity. But just as Mr. Beardsley with all his absurdities is none the less a master of black and white, so Mr. Crane is a true poet whose verse, long after the eccentricity of its form has worn off, fascinates us and forbids us to lay the volume down until the last line has been read.

Professor Peck concluded that Crane was not a decadent, but a "bold—sometimes too bold—original, and powerful writer of

---

pleasant controversy centered around Crane's morality, creating the atmosphere that would lead to charges of sexual misbehavior, narcotics addiction, and drunkenness during the Dora Clark affair. See Olov W. Fryckstedt, "Stephen Crane in the Tenderloin," *Studia Neophilologica.* XXXIV (1962), 135-163.

eccentric verse, skeptical, pessimistic, often cynical." Nevertheless, the tactic provided a tag for contemporary reviewers, and a vision for some later critics.[35]

The comparison between Crane's techniques and those of Walt Whitman was as immediate as the identification with the decadents. "In fact," said the *Bookman,* if Walt Whitman had been caught young and subjected to aesthetic influences, it is likely that he would have mellowed his barbaric yawp to some such note as that which sounds in the poems that are now before us."[36] Despite the protest of Horace Traubel's *Conservator,* an organ devoted to the outpourings of the Whitman apostles, contempory reviewers considered the comparison both valid and useful.[37] Usually, however, they agreed with Jeanette L. Gilder's judgment that "We may have pardoned Walt Whitman's shortcoming in this direction for the sake of his poetic thoughts, but we cannot go on forgiving these eccentricities of genius forever."[38]

Not all comments on *The Black Riders* were serious attempts at definition or criticism. The nineties were gay in many ways, perhaps most gay in their embrace of parody and satire, and Crane's first volume of verse attracted both scornful and friendly fun. Even the enthusiastic *Bookman* could follow its extravagant praise of Crane's art with a parody beginning "I explain the crooked track of a coon at night,"

---

[34] Peck, "Some Recent Volumes of Verse," *Bookman,* I (May 1895), 254.

[35] The popular *Handbook to Literature* (New York, 1960) by Thrall, Hibbard, and Holman concludes its note on the *decadents* by stating that "there are decadent qualities in Stephen Crane."

[36] Peck, "Some Recent Volumes of Verse."

[37] Isaac Hull Platt, "The Black Riders," *Conservator,* VI (July 1895), 78.

[38] Gilder, "Stephen Crane's Study of War," New York *World,* 23 February 1896, p. 18, is a review of *The Red Badge* and a retrospective consideration of Crane's career. A notable exception to the Gilder position was the review in the *Times* (London), 4 February 1897, p. 7.

and Elbert Hubbard—soon to feast Crane—could deliver a mocking review of the book.[39]

Messrs. Copeland & Day of Boston recently published for Mr. Stephen Crane a book which he called "The Black Riders." I don't know why; the riders might have as easily been green or yellow or baby-blue for all the book tells about them, and I think the title "The Pink Roosters" would have been better, but it doesn't matter. My friend, The Onlooker, of *Town Topics,* quotes one of the verses and says this, which I heartily endorse:

> I saw a man pursuing the horizon;
> Round and round they sped.
> I was disturbed at this;
> I accosted the man.
> "It is futile," I said,
> "You can never"—
> "You lie," he cried.
> And ran on.

This was Mr. Howells proving that Ibsen is valuable and interesting. It is to be hoped that Mr. Crane will write another poem about him after his legs have been worn off.

Five months later, Hubbard invited Crane to accept a dinner in his honor, and six months after that he inaugurated the *Roycroft Quarterly* with a commemoration of the banquet— and the first poem in that issue was the very poem he ridiculed. Even while Crane was regularly contributing poetry to the *Philistine,* Hubbard was equally ready to devote a prominent page to Crane's lines or to a parody of those lines.

---

[39] W. S. Bean, "Lines after Stephen Crane," *Bookman,* IV (December, 1896), 332; Hubbard, [Review of *The Black Riders*], *Philistine,* I (June 1895), 27.

III "A MAN BUILDED A BUGLE FOR THE STORMS TO BLOW"

Despite the sparse mixture of reviews that greeted *The Black Riders,* Crane soon earned the reputation for being "a wonderful boy." While he had been negotiating for the book of poems, *The Red Badge of Courage* had been syndicated in the newspapers (in much abbreviated form), and the respect that it had earned won it a contract with D. Appleton and Company.[40] While reviewers might still look back on *The Black Riders* with some disdain, they nevertheless did look back. And as the sales of *The Red Badge* soared, Crane's work came into demand.

Surprisingly, it was Elbert Hubbard who—in contrast to the attitude of his silly review of *The Black Riders*— was one of the first to detect Crane's growing importance and to offer him a steady outlet for his poems.[41] Though the July, 1895, *Philistine* printed a parody that lacerated Crane's poetic techniques, the August and September issues carried two poems (*94, 101*) that Copeland and Day evidently had not seen. On the surface it might appear that Hubbard's endorsement marked a break between Crane and the *avant garde* that Hubbard opposed (and with whom Crane had been identified). Amy Lowell, for example, looked back in shock: "It was difficult for the world to believe that a man championed

---

[40] *The Red Badge* first appeared in the Philadelphia *Press,* 3-8 December 1894, pp. 11; 9; 10; 13; 11. The New York newspapers carried the piece a few days later.

[41] The most reliable survey of Crane's publication in Hubbard's periodical is David H. Dickason, "Stephen Crane and the *Philistine,*" *American Literature,* XV (November 1943), 279-287.

I Explain the silvered path of a ship at night
The sweep of each sad lost wave
The dwindling boom of the steel thing's striving
The little cry of a man to a man
~~Then The~~ The shadow falling across the
greyer night
And the sinking of the small star.

~~Then, the silence~~
Then the waste, the far waste waters
And the soft lashing of black waves.
For long and in lonliness.

~~Explain~~
Oh, thou, my ship
Remember, thou, in thy stern straight.

Thou leavest a waste, a waste of far <sup>journey</sup>

And the soft lashing of black <sup>waters</sup> ~~waters~~
For long and in lonliness.

Draft Q: "I Explain the silvered path of a ship at night" (81).
Facsimile of the manuscript in the Syracuse University Library.

by the arch-poser, Elbert Hubbard, could have merit."[42] But the road to success makes for strange companions, and Hubbard did, after all, share a common inspiration with Copeland and Day, Stone and Kimball, the *Bookman* people, and the rest of the Crane enthusiasts.

Early in the last decade of the nineteenth century, Hubbard visited England and William Morris. In the words of Felix Shay, Hubbard's employee and biographer,

When Hubbard came a-visiting, Morris was getting on toward sixty, while Hubbard was still in his middle thirties. The difference in ages made it easy for one to give and the other to take; one, in a sense, became the grateful apostle of the other. Morris tossed the torch to the hand that was ready to grasp it, and Hubbard said he "caught it!"[43]

If Hubbard's grasp was faulty, there was still a haze of the theories and ideal of William Morris surrounding his early operations. Despite his failure "to grasp the fundamentals of this thought,"[44] Hubbard did have an influence on the *kultur* of his day and an influence on Stephen Crane's career.

" 'East Aurora,' said Hubbard, 'is not a place; it's a state of mind.' "[45] The Roycroft Community in East Aurora, New York, resulted from Hubbard's exploitation of Morris's retreat into communal industry based on handicraft. The state of mind transformed a small, upper New York State village

---

[42] Amy Lowell's Introduction to *The Work of Stephen Crane*, (New York, 1926), VI, xxiii.

[43] Felix Shay, *Elbert Hubbard of East Aurora* (New York, 1926), p. 31.

[44] The estimate of Hubbard in James D. Hart, *The Oxford Companion to American Literature*, Third Edition (New York, 1956), p. 342, while seemingly harsh, is probably fair.

[45] Shay, *Elbert Hubbard*, p. 53.

into a group of moderately skillful artificers who produced mission style furnishings and who designed, printed (and occasionally illuminated), and bound books fashioned along the lines of the Kelmscott Press productions.[46] While a few of the titles in the catalog of the Roycroft Press were first printings of authors discovered by Hubbard, many were reprintings of the standard works of the time, but most were publications of the works of Elbert Hubbard. Throughout his operations, Hubbard maintained just the right posture of staid bohemianism that would pique the interest of the slightly daring businessman. In many senses, Hubbard was the founder of modern American advertising.

These characteristics of the Hubbard touch are apparent in the most successful of the Roycroft ventures, the *Philistine*. Purporting to be the organ of a Society of the Philistines, the periodical was begun in June, 1895, and delivered monthly comments on life and the arts in a tone of which the review of *The Black Riders* is representative. In Crane, Hubbard saw a cause and a good thing, and he invited the author of *The Black Riders* to be guest of honor at the first annual dinner of the Society of the Philistines.

"Recognizing in yourself and in your genius as a poet, a man who we would like to know better," the invitation began, "The Society of the Philistines desire to give a dinner in your honor early in the future." "I was very properly enraged at the word 'poet' which continually reminds me of long-hair and seems to me to be a most detestable form of insult but nevertheless I replied," Crane later wrote.[47] Naively, he wondered

---

[46] Theodore Dreiser's comments in *A Hoosier Holiday* (New York, 1916), pp. 141-44, 163-68, record his disgust with the "state of mind" of East Aurora. After a short time spent in viewing Hubbard's town, Dreiser fled.

[47] The invitation and Crane's summary of the events at the dinner are printed in a letter to Nellie Crouse in E. H. Cady and Lester G. Wells,

whether he was honored because he had written "for their magazine" and he was overwhelmed by feelings of "pride and arrogance to think that I have such friends."[48] But the dinner was not quite what he had anticipated. Although Hubbard had declared that Crane represented a " 'cause' " and that the Philistines wished "in a dignified, public (and at the same time) elegant manner to recognize that cause," Crane stood in borrowed clothing and was "roasted" by a group of "freaks or near-freaks."[49]

Shocked, one of the guests began to leave, but he was stopped by Crane and by Crane's close friend and benefactor, Willis Brooks Hawkins. This was undoubtedly wise, for Hubbard supplied Crane with a steady outlet for his work and Crane would have lost much by alienating Hubbard. On the day of the dinner, for example, Hubbard issued elaborate souvenir menus—*"The Time Has Come," The Walrus Said, "To Talk of Many Things"* (Publication 5) —which provided the first publication of "I have heard the sunset song of the birches" (*82*), and several months later he printed a souvenir booklet of the occasion, *A Souvenir and a Medley*, the first issue of the *Roycroft Quarterly* (Publication 13). In *A Souvenir and a Medley*, Hubbard got double-mileage out of Crane's writings: six poems—all that had appeared in the *Philistine* to that date—were reprinted here, while he anticipated the June *Philistine* printing of "Fast rode the knight" (*83*) by first printing it in this volume.

---

*Stephen Crane's Love Letters to Nellie Crouse* (Syracuse, New York, 1954), pp. 25-27.

[48] *Letters*, pp. 74, 73.

[49] Hubbard to Crane, 16 November 1895, in *Letters*, p. 75; Frank Noxon's report of the gathering of "freaks or near-freaks" printed in *Love Letters to Nellie Crouse*, pp. 63-69, and Claude F. Bragdon's "The Purple Cow Period," *Bookman*, LXIX (July 1928), 478, indicate—probably with much justice—that the affair was tasteless and offensive.

In all, Hubbard published twenty-one of Crane's poems—many more than once—and provided the major periodical outlet for Crane's verse. Two poems were printed in the *Philistine* in the first four months of its publication, and the first poem was printed just two months after Hubbard's comic review of *The Black Riders*. While Crane's lines appeared in almost every issue of the *Philistine* during the period from August, 1895, to June, 1896, no poems were printed in the issues of from July, 1896, to February, 1898. From February, 1898, through December, 1898, five poems by Crane saw first printing in the *Philistine*, and two poems were reprinted in 1899. The tapering-off may be explained in part by Crane's travels, in part by his development of other, more congenial, outlets, (the *Chap-Book* and the *Bookman*) for his poems, in part by Hubbard's "democratic prejudice against royalties,"[50] and in part by Hubbard's lack of taste, his deficient understanding of the nature of art, and his grotesque use of a near-tragedy as an occasion for advertising. On 1 January 1897, Crane was on the *Commodore,* a vessel that was sunk while carrying arms and ammunition to Cuban rebels. He was missing until 3 January and was thought dead. The close contact with death greatly affected him, and he attempted to write it out in a newspaper report and in "The Open Boat" and "Flanagan and His Short Filibustering Adventure." The scars show still more lividly in his attitudes toward the sea in his poetry, especially in "A man adrift on a slim spar" (*113*) . Hubbard's writing about Crane's experience was at best insensitive. In the February, 1897, issue of the *Philistine,* he printed a lachrymose obituary in which he reported Crane's

---

[50] Frank Noxon suspected that Crane broke with Hubbard over the question of royalties. See *Love Letters to Nellie Crouse*, p. 69. But if there really was a rupture, the break was not complete.

death by drowning—followed, a few pages after by "LATER: Thanks to Providence and a hen coop, Steve Crane was not drowned after all—he swam ashore." Equally irritating is Hubbard's heavy touch in regularizing and even rewriting the verse of Crane that appeared in the *Philistine*.

While neither the *Chap-Book* with its one Crane poem, nor the *Bookman* with its twelve (two reprinted from *The Black Riders*; three first printed posthumously) provided as large an outlet as did Hubbard, they are at least as significant indications of the measure of Crane's acceptance. During the editorship of Harry Thurston Peck, a former Columbia University faculty member, the *Bookman* was extremely influential as an advanced—but respectable—literary journal; and, no doubt through his direction, the periodical practiced the sort of puffing that is faintly reminiscent of Hubbard's methods—save, of course, that it was tasteful. For in addition to avowed reviews of Crane's verse, "Chronicle and Comment" would occasionally drop Crane's name before its readers. On the first page of the March, 1896, number for example, the *Bookman* commented on *Jude the Obscure* by suggesting that Crane's "In the desert" (3) would serve well as an epigraph for Hardy's novel. But the chief value of these two periodicals was neither in their payment nor in their puffery; they were most significant in demonstrating to Crane that he was acceptable as a poet to discriminating, quality magazines. Here was enthusiasm from translators, not prostitutes, of Morrisean publishing ideals. And occasional reprinting in the New York *Times*, in the literary digests, and in such a mass-circulation volume as Sidney Witherbee's *Spanish-American War Songs* (Publication 23) could serve only to encourage Crane as a poet.

When one adds this periodical success to Crane's own statement that "Personally, I like my little book of poems, 'The

Black Riders,' better than I do 'The Red Badge of Courage',"
one is left with a sense of bewilderment at the small body of
verse that survives.[51] To some degree this can be explained by
Crane's carelessness. After all, he did leave "All-feeling God,
hear in the war-night" (*129*) with Charles Michelson in his
Spanish-American War saddlebags, and they were returned to
his widow only one month after his death.[52] But there are
other, more important reasons for the slimness of the canon.

When W. D. Howells attempted to dissuade Crane from
writing the "prose poem," when he remarked on the "simple,
but always most graphic" terms in which *Maggie* was ex-
pressed, and when he printed one of the poems in *The Black
Riders* as prose, he was pointing towards Crane's exceptional
ability to bring the rhythms of prose and poetry close to-
gether.[53] For if Crane was not entirely satisfied to "quench the
old rage and satisfy the old commitment in stories" (as Mor-
gan Blum has offered,[54] he was exceptionally able to integrate
into his fiction the rhythms and themes on which his poetry
depends: the parallel suggested by Howells was extended by
Melvin Schoberlin's printing of excerpts from the prose as
poetry.[55] But though Crane was able to draw the rhythmic
modes together, though he could utilize similar themes and
episodes in both fiction and poetry, it was the burning need of

---

[51] Crane to John Northern Hilliard, [1897?], in *Letters,* p. 159.

[52] Gilkes, *Cora Crane* (Bloomington, Indiana, 1960), p. 288n.

[53] *Letters,* p. 40; Howells, "New York Low Life in Fiction," New York
*World,* 26 July 1896, p. 18 and "An Appreciation," in *Maggie* (London, 1896);
Howells, "[Review of *The Black Riders*]."

[54] Blum, "Berryman as Biographer, Stephen Crane as Poet," *Poetry,*
LXXVIII (August 1951), 307.

[55] Melvin Schoberlin, *The Sullivan County Sketches,* (Syracuse, New York,
1949), p. 13.

money rather than the quenching of artistic rage that assured a small poetic output.[56]

H. G. Wells's horror at "a medley of impulsive disproportionate expenditure" displayed by the Cranes at a Christmas party in England is indicative of the shameful waste of time, energy, and money in which Cora and Stephen indulged themselves.[57] In an attempt to keep but slightly behind his creditors, Crane ground out short stories at a phenomenal rate, forcing his English agent to plead for a reduction of the pressure to sell, sell, sell. "There is a risk of spoiling the

---

[56] The duplication of incident in Crane's poetry and fiction has never been properly explored. The most striking of these "twins" appears in *Maggie* and in "With eye and with gesture" (*57*). Pete has just shrugged off Maggie, answering her "But where kin I go?" with "Oh, go teh hell." The girl walks the streets distractedly:

> Suddenly she came upon a stout gentleman in a silk hat and a chaste black coat, whose decorous row of buttons reached from his chin to his knees. The girl had heard of the Grace of God and she decided to approach this man.
>
> His beaming, chubby face was a picture of benevolence and kind-heartedness. His eyes shone good-will.
>
> But as the girl timidly accosted him, he gave a convulsive movement and saved his respectability by a vigorous side-step. He did not risk it to save a soul. For how was he to know that there was a soul before him that needed saving?

In *The Black Riders,* the incident is more compressed, the judgment more explicit:

With eye and with gesture
You say you are holy.
I say you lie;
For I did see you
Draw away your coats
From the sin upon the hands
Of a little child.
Liar!

[57] H. G. Wells, *Experiment in Autobiography* (New York, 1934), p. 524.

market if we have to dump too many short stories on it at once."[58] Ironically, since the laws of economics are not suspended for authors in need, Pinker's prediction came true: as Crane flooded the market with his short stories, the rate of pay dwindled.[59] And the mill ground faster but worse.

The sheer bulk of the short fiction eventually looked to overwhelm the gradually fewer pieces of quality, and did of course overwhelm the poetry. And yet the dwindling of the poetic output allows the direction of Crane's poetry to come into clearer focus. It had always been dramatic in conception. The journey motif within *The Black Riders* is essentially a dramatic concept, and the poems for which that motif provides continuity are dramatic in execution. Crane's frequent gestures toward writing for the stage which culminated disappointingly in "The Ghost," and which were marked by occasional pastiches on the order of "A Prologue," are quite relevant to a discussion of his aesthetic.[60]

---

[58] James B. Pinker to Crane, 24 October 1899, in *Letters*, p. 236.

[59] See James B. Stronks, "Stephen Crane's English Years: The Legend Corrected," *Papers of the Bibliographical Society of America*, LVII (Third Quarter, 1963), 340-349.

[60] In September, 1895, Crane thought he would be doing dramatic criticism for the Philadelphia *Press*, but the offer of the job was quickly withdrawn (see *Letters*, p. 63). Actually, he had published odds and ends of dramatic criticism at various times: "Some Hints for Play-Makers," *Truth*, 28 October 1893; "Miss Louise Gerard—Soprano," *Musical News*, December, 1894; "Grand Opera in New Orleans," Philadelphia *Press*, 24 March, 1895, part 3, p. 25; "At the Pit Door," *Philistine*, XI (September 1900), 97-104. These have all been reprinted in Olov W. Fryckstedt, *Stephen Crane: Uncollected Writings* (Uppsala, 1963).

In early 1898, Crane proposed to Joseph Conrad that they collaborate on a play to be called *The Predecessor*. Conrad recalled (Beer, *Stephen Crane*, pp. 29-30):

The general subject consisted in a man personating his "predecessor" (who had died) in the hope of winning a girl's heart. The scenes were to include

As in his "plays," his "sketches," and his "scenes," many of the poems in *The Black Riders* depend on a clash of two or more voices. Thomas Wentworth Higginson praised the book for offering "points-of-view" of a situation, and in this he was nodding towards just that technique of collision. Frequently, the major voice is that of the persona reporting an incident which he had seen ("In the desert | I saw a creature, naked, bestial" *3*) or of which he had learned ("Once there came a man | Who said: | 'Range me all men of the world in rows." *5*) or in which he had participated ("A learned man came to me once" *20*) . The second voice—occasionally the other voices —usually represents some viewpoint which is revealed as inferior. In the clash, a dominant attitude emerges. "Preaching is fatal to art in literature," Crane had self-consciously said to

---

a ranch at the foot of the Rocky Mountains, I remember, and the action I fear would have been frankly melodramatic. Crane insisted that one of the situations should present the man and the girl on a boundless plain standing by their dead ponies after a furious ride (a truly Crane touch) . I made some objections. A boundless plain in the light of a sunset could be got into a back-cloth, I admitted; but I doubted whether we could induce the management of any London theatre to deposit two stuffed horses on its stage.

But Crane did pursue the dramatic urges that led him to do "A Prologue," *Roycroft Quarterly*, I (May 1896) , 38. In addition to the ironic "The Blood of the Martyr," New York *Press, Sunday Magazine*, I (3 April 1898) , 9-11, he conceived of "The Ghost," a play that he based on a spirit that was said to haunt Brede Place. This was given as an entertainment for the villagers of Brede in Christmas, 1899. Crane wrote the play, and had Conrad, Henry James, H. G. Wells and other, less noted, authors insert a word or a phrase so that he could state that they were all collaborators in the comedy. See John D. Gordan, *"The Ghost* at Brede Place,"*Bulletin of the New York Public Library*, LVI (December 1952) , 591-596. In addition to this "awful rubbish," Columbia University Library has the first act of a play set in a French tavern, and some acts and the dramatis personae of a Spanish-American War play. (See also R. W. Stallman and E. R. Hagemann, *The War Dispatches of Stephen Crane* (New York, 1964) , pp. 315-334.)

John Northern Hilliard. "I try to give readers a slice out of life; and if there is any moral or lesson in it, I do not try to point it out. I let the reader find it for himself. The result is more satisfactory to both the reader and myself."[61] The failures in *The Black Riders* might well be attributed to the harshness that is occasionally noted in effecting the dominance of the developed attitude.

While Crane retained the device in many of the later poems, he came to develop a firm grasp of his technique that tended to soften the "preachiness." "A man said to the universe" (*96*) certainly echoes, but it is effective because the earlier technique has been sophisticated and not because the poem is "simple." This sophistication was carried further into an experimentation with the refrain and with the opposition of stanza patterns. On the surface this might appear to be but a movement from the tradition of the parable into the highly formal structures symptomatic of the contemporary mainstream; actually, the movement is also a further step into the dramatic. As in "Do not weep, maiden, for war is kind" (*76*) and "All-feeling God, hear in the war-night" (*129*), the opposition of stanzas and the use of the refrain serve to introduce a choric counterpoint. The consistence of that counterpoint contrasts with the diffusion of what would otherwise be the major voice to develop the dominant attitude, and the result—in the more successful poems—is a subtlety that distinguishes *War Is Kind* from the early volume.

If Crane could occasionally submerge himself in the opetry in an attempt to recapture the artistic satisfaction that he was frequently forced to abdicate in the prose, he was nevertheless finally forced to transmute the verse into money. This is one of the keys to an otherwise puzzling volume. The creation of

---

[61] Crane to Hilliard, [1897?], *Letters*, pp. 158-59.

*The Black Riders* was marked by a coherence brought about by an intensity of composition, and the publication of the volume was surrounded by a similar violent protective urge that is apparent in the correspondence between Crane and Copeland and Day. The aura around *War Is Kind* partakes rather of the quality of gleaning than sowing, and is dominated by the careless off-handedness that Crane assumed in closing a business affair. Frederick A. Stokes Company, through its London representative, had advanced Crane money, had made him loans, and had guaranteed his debts.[62] In an obvious attempt to repay this obligation, Crane collected many of his periodically published poems, surrendering them to Stokes as *War Is Kind.*

The commercial qualities are apparent in the composition of the book. Only the embarrassingly tedious "Intrigue" cycle and twelve of the individual poems are first printings. Of the twelve poems, no more than nine could have been written for the volume: two poems *(78, 91)* were among those rejected by Copeland and Day from *The Black Riders,* and a fragment of one *(79)* had been sent in 1896 or 1897 to Elbert Hubbard for publication in the *Philistine* (it was not printed by Hubbard until 1910, when he reproduced the poem in another periodical). The occasionally Whitmanian "Intrigue" had been written while Crane was in Cuba in 1898, and had been offered to William Heinemann as—evidently—a slim volume to be composed of one stanza to a page.[63] But while Heinemann had served as the English publisher of *The Black Riders* and other volumes, they declined "Intrigue." To reinforce the

---

62 For example, Stokes had indicated that it would guarantee at least a portion of a debt that had been outstanding for about two years. See Crane to James B. Pinker, 4 February 1899, *Letters,* pp. 207-08.

63 Crane to Paul Revere Reynolds, 20 October [1898], *Letters,* p. 189.

commercial air, Crane neatly noted in his typescript the place of original appearance of each of the reprintings, and then—without noting that it had appeared in *The Black Riders,* probably because he went back to the original manuscript as the source of this text of the poem—used as a filler "There was one I met upon the road" *(33, 99)*.

*War Is Kind* was copyrighted in April, 1899, and was announced for sale in May.[64] The tall, grey-paper volume shouted "decadence" at its audience, and reinforced the tag that had been applied to Crane four years earlier. And yet, he had probably had no hand in selecting the format, no decision in the choice of Will Bradley, the artist whose Beardsleyesque illustrations contributed to the *fin de siecle* atmosphere, and evidently no participation in the correcting of proof. Only when Edmund Clarence Stedman asked for some poems for inclusion in his important *American Anthology* (Publication 27) did Crane even refer to the book in his correspondence.[65] But life was dribbling away. In his concern with debt, physical weakness, the loss of satisfaction with the relation of his life and his art, Crane had feebly responded to the honor

---

[64] It is quite probable that Sidney Pawling of Heinemann retained the copy of Crane's typescript of *War Is Kind* that he was considering as late as February, 1899 (see Crane to Pinker, 4 February 1899, *Letters,* p. 207). *The Windmill* (1923), a collection of short pieces by the authors of "the many books which have been issued by the Heinemann firm" (p. v), contains "What Says the Sea, Little Shell" (77) and "To the Maiden" (78). Heinemann had gone so far in its consideration of the book as to prepare, according to Williams and Starrett, *Stephen Crane: A Bibliography,* p. 41, six copies to secure English copyright.

*War is Kind* was reviewed by the Springfield *Republican,* 4 June 1899, p. 12; *Bookman,* IX (July 1899), 466; Thomas Wentworth Higginson, *Nation,* LXIX (16 November 1899), 378; Rupert Hughes, "Mr. Crane's Crazyquilting," *Criterion,* XXI (3 June 1899), 26-27.

[65] Crane to Stedman, 4 September 1899, *Letters,* p. 229.

1

that the important critic had accorded him with an incorrect statement that every poem he had ever written would be found in his two published volumes. The young man of twenty-three who could jibe at his tongue of wood, was shattered into the parodist of Longfellow, feebly protesting at the end of his brief career as a poet:

> Tell me not in joyous numbers
> We can make our lives sublime
> By—well, at least, not by
> Dabbling much in rhyme.

# Textual Introduction

The text of this edition of Stephen Crane's poetry is based on the axiom that any act of selection is in reality an act of criticism, and as such should derive from communicable critical principles. These principles will apply, in a broad sense, to both the postulation of the canon and to the establishment of the texts of the poems within that canon.

While poems, poem fragments, near-poems, parodies, and adaptions of poems that have been incorporated into Crane's prose writings will be of interest to the student of his poetry, these must all be omitted from the canon on the grounds that they have been shaped by concerns that are extrinsic to the concerns of the poet. The rejected pieces are in the following, collected in volumes of *The Work of Stephen Crane*, ed. Wilson Follett (New York, 1925-27): *The Red Badge of Courage* (I: pp. 88, 151); "The Monster" (III: pp. 54, 68, 204); *The Third Violet* (III; p. 200); "Making an Orator" (V: pp. 66, 70-71); *The O'Ruddy* (VII: p. 52); "The Sergeant's Private Madhouse" (IX: pp. 116-17); *George's Mother* (X: pp. 24-25, 52); "The Auction" (XI: p. 80); "The Five White Mice" (XII: pp. 161, 172). Into the same excluded category fall several pieces not in the *Work* which have been collected in Olov W. Fryckstedt's *Stephen Crane: Uncollected Writings* (Uppsala, 1963): "Heard in the Street Election Night" (pp. 86-89); "A Christmas Dinner Won in Battle" (p. 108); "A Lovely Jag" (p. 112); "At the Pit Door" (pp. 446-47). Two poems used as epigraphs to prose writings—"A soldier, young in years, young in ambitions" (*124*), and "Unwind my riddle" (*117*) —do not fall into this category and have therefore been included in the canon.

All poems in *The Black Riders and Other Lines* and *War Is Kind* have unquestionable right to be included in the canon, as have all poems that survive in Crane's holograph, in his typescript, or in proof corrected by him. In addition, poems which have appeared below Crane's name in the periodicals to which he had regularly contributed have been admitted to the canon. Special note must be made of two poems in this category that survive in no other form: It is quite possible that Elbert Hubbard might have undertaken to write and to publish as Crane's "Rumbling, buzzing, turning, whirling Wheels" (*75*) on the front wrapper of the *Philistine* (Publication 22) as a means of advertising his association with the poet. But the similarity of this poem to "A grey and boiling street" (*130*) has warranted its inclusion in the canon. "Legends" (*69-73*), which appeared in the *Bookman* (Publication 14) during Crane's extended absence from the United States, is included with less suspicion because of the reputability of that periodical.

"All-feeling God, hear in the war-night" (*129*) would ordinarily be included in the canon with much suspicion since it survives only in a copy prepared by Cora Crane. An examination of her procedure in preparing copies of Crane's poems, however, indicates that while she was prone to the textual ailments of many nineteenth century editors, she nevertheless tended to be faithful to what she understood to be Crane's final intentions. The text of this poem must however be considered less than ultimately desirable. For a detailed discussion of the procedure used in evaluating Cora's participation in this poem, see Katz, "Cora Crane and the Poetry of Stephen Crane."

The establishment of the texts of the poems in the canon has been based on the discernible degree of authority of the documents. All of the available draft materials prepared by Crane have been collated, and "family trees" of the poems have been established. Because of the close relationship between Cora Crane and Crane's writings (especially because he "ghosted" several pieces that appeared under her name and because she acted as his business manager, his amanuensis, and his posthumous collaborator) the copies that she prepared of the poems have been collated.

Any published document that has an intrinsic claim to significance has been collated and examined for authority. Such a claim might derive from the probability of Crane's participation in the publication (Publications 1, 3-6, 8-16, 18-22, 24, 28); from the possibility that, because it is either contemporaneous with Crane or derivative from authoritative sources, the document records authoritative variants (Publications 2, 7, 17, 23, 25, 26, 29); from the document being a first, although posthumous, publication (Publications 31, 33, 34); or from the historical significance of the document as a traditional source of the texts of the poems (Publications 27, 30, 32). Obvious reprintings in periodicals such as the *Literary Digest* which have none of the stated claims to significance have been omitted from the collations. Similarly, private reprintings "for the friends of" the issuers, a species of publication that aspires to an authority that it rarely evidences, have been examined but have been omitted from the collations. The more important of these reprintings have been considered in the Notes.

## THE BLACK RIDERS AND OTHER LINES

Manuscripts of only five poems in this volume survive (Drafts A-E), and these have been collated. In addition, seven

# THE BLACK RIDERS AND OTHER LINES BY STEPHEN CRANE

BOSTON COPELAND AND DAY MDCCCXCV

Facsimile of the title page of the first impression of *The Black Riders and Other Lines* (Publication 1). Reproduced from the copy in the Butler Library of Columbia University.

publications constituting four editions of *The Black Riders* have been collated. Four publications (Publications 1, 2, 7, and 17) authorized by Copeland and Day, the original publishers of the volume, appeared during Crane's lifetime and constitute the first edition. The remaining editions (Publications 29, 30, and 32) were issued by successors to the copyright after Crane's death.

Publications 1 and 2 constitute the first impression of the first edition, and collate as follows:

(*Title*, p. [i]) : THE BLACK RIDERS AND | OTHER LINES BY STE- | PHEN CRANE | BOSTON COPELAND AND DAY MDCCCXCV

(*Copyright notice*, p. [ii]): ENTERED ACCORDING TO THE ACT OF CONGRESS | IN THE YEAR MDCCCXCV BY COPELAND AND DAY | IN THE OFFICE OF THE LIBRARIAN OF CONGRESS | AT WASHINGTON

(*Dedication*, p. [iii]) : TO HAMLIN GARLAND

(*Printer's imprint*, p. [77]) : PRINTED BY JOHN WILSON AND SON CAMBRIDGE

(*Collation*): (6 1/8 x 4 1/4 inches) : [unsigned: A² B-F⁸]; 42 leaves, pp. [i-iv] 1-76 [77-80].

(*Contents*) : p. [i], title; p. [ii], copyright notice; p. [iii], dedication; p. [iv], blank; [poems in the volume headed by numerals I-LXVIII; reference here is by poem number in this edition of Crane's poems] p. 1, *1*; p. 2, *2*; p. 3, *3*; p. 4, *4*; p. 5, *5*; pp. 6-7, *6*; p. 8, *7*; p. 9, *8*; p. 10, *9*; p. 11, *10*; p. 12, *11*; p. 13, *12*; p. 14, *13*; p. 15, *14*; p. 16, *15*; p. 17, *16*; p. 18, *17*; p. 19, *18*; p. 20, *19*; p. 21, *20*; p. 22, *21;* p. 23, *22*; p. 24, *23;* p. 25, *24*; p. 26, *25*; p. 27, *26*; p. 28, *27*; p. 29, *28*; p. 30, *29*; p. 31, *30*; p. 32, *31*; p. 33, *32*; p. 34, *33*; p.35, *34*; p. 36, *35*; p. 37, *36*; p. 38, *37*; pp. 39-40, *38*; p. 41, *39*; pp. 42-43, *40*; p. 44, *41;* p. 45, *42;* p. 46, *43;* p. 47, *44;* p. 48, *45;* p. 49, *46;* p. 50, *47*; p. 51, *48*; pp. 52-54, *49*; p. 55, *50*; p. 56, *51*; p. 57, *52*; pp. 58-59, *53*; p. 60, *54*; p. 61, *55*; p. 62, *56*; p. 63, *57;*

p. 64, *58*; p. 65, *59*; p. 66, *60*; pp. 67-68, *61*; p. 69, *62*; p. 70, *63*; p. 71, *64*; p. 72, *65*; p. 73, *66*; p. 74, *67*; pp. 75-76, *68*; p. [77], printer's imprint; pp. [78-80], blank.

(*Typography and paper*) : 18 lines (leaded), 3 (3 1/2) x 2 1/2 (p. 6) ; 6 pt. roman caps with 6 pt. leading throughout text. White wove unwatermarked paper; fore-edge unopened, top and bottom edges cut; sheets bulk 1/2."

(*Binding*) : Printed white boards. Front: [set flush left] THE BLACK RIDERS | AND OTHER | LINES | BY | STEPHEN | CRANE | [orchid design]. Spine: THE | BLACK | RIDERS | STEPHEN | CRANE | COPELAND | AND | DAY | 1895. The lettering of the back is identical with that of the front; the orchid design is a mirror-image of that of the front. All printing and decoration is in black. Gatherings of four leaves of book stock are used as pastedowns and binder's leaves at the front and back. Stamped on the front pastedown is the binder's imprint: DUDLEY & HODGE.

Publication 2 is a variant printing in green ink on Japan paper. Within this printing are two binding variants. Binding Variant 1: Cream laid paper, paper label on the spine lettered as follows: [double rule] | THE | BLACK | RIDERS | [rule] | CRANE | [rule] | 1895 | [double rule]. Binding Variant 2 is bound in white vellum stamped in gold. Williams and Starrett, *Stephen Crane: A Bibliography*, p. 17, note an additional variant in the binding of the green ink printing of the first impression: "bound in full green levant by Cobden-Sanderson, stamped 'The Doves Bindery, 18 C-S 96.' inside the back cover." This might be one of the two variant bindings within the major printing noted in Jacob Blanck, *Bibliography of American Literature,* Volume II, p. 329, as in publisher's leather and in printed blue-grey laid paper boards (both in the Clifton Waller Barrett collection) .

Both the major black ink printing of the first impression

lviii

and the minor green ink printing were advertised in *Publishers' Weekly,* 9 February 1895, as appearing shortly in an edition "limited to five hundred copies, with fifty copies additional printed in green ink on Japan paper." The Williams and Starrett (p. 17) suggestion that the green ink variant is an edition may be disregarded on two counts. First, the variant was announced at the same time as the major run, in a prospectus issued by Copeland and Day between 6 January and 14 January 1895.[1] And less than a few weeks after the date of publication of the first edition (the edition was published on 30 March 1895), Crane asked Copeland and Day for "the green ones."[2] Second, incontrovertible evidence that the variant is of the same edition as Publication 1 is supplied by an error common to both publications. In both, the terminal punctuation of the eighth line of "Friend, your white beard sweeps the ground" (*64*) appears as a question mark. This compositor's error was subsequently revised to an exclamation point, and the substitution is retained in succeeding impressions of the first edition. (But note that the revision probably did not come from Crane's manuscript, since that had undoubtedly been returned to him before the second impression was prepared.) Similarly, while Publications 1 and 2 record Crane's spelling "gayly" (*61*), Publications 7 and 17 produce the more common "gaily."

On 27 September 1894, Crane agreed to accept a ten per cent royalty on the book.[3] The black ink copies were an-

---

[1] Crane to Copeland and Day, *Letters*, pp. 47, 48, first supplied reviews of *Maggie* for quotation, then asked for additional copies of the prospectus. Copies of the prospectus are in Columbia University Libraries.

[2] Crane to Copeland and Day, [June ? 1895], *Letters,* p. 59.

[3] Crane to Copeland and Day, quoted in Joan H. Baum, *Stephen Crane (1871-1900): An Exhibition of His Writings Held in the Columbia University Libraries* (New York, [1956]), p. 20. The letter is in the Barrett collection of the Alderman Library.

nounced at a price of $1.00, while the fifty green ink copies were priced at $3.00. His request in May, 1895, for a settlement of *The Black Riders* account lends weight to the belief that he played little part in preparing the second impression, Publication 7.[4]

The dedication, the printer's imprint, and the collation of the second impression are identical with those of the first impression. The contents are identical with those of the first impression except for uneven attempts at substituting *-our* for *-or* endings in the texts of several poems, and for the corrections noted above. The title-page and the copyright page have been reset:

(*Title*, p. [i]: THE BLACK RIDERS AND | OTHER LINES BY STE- | PHEN CRANE | BOSTON COPELAND AND DAY MDCCCXCVI | LONDON WILLIAM HEINEMANN

(*Copyright notice*, p. [ii]) : THIRD EDITION | ENTERED ACCORDING TO THE ACT OF CONGRESS | IN THE YEAR MDCCCXCVI BY COPELAND AND DAY | IN THE OFFICE OF THE LIBRARIAN OF CONGRESS | AT WASHINGTON

The reset pages and the Anglicisations reflect the co-operative issuance of the volume in England and America. In all probability, the joint publication was called forth by the great success in England of *The Red Badge of Courage*. Heinemann had issued the English edition of *The Red Badge* in November, 1895. Haste is evident in the carelessness of the orthographical revisions; these are significant enough to suggest that they were carried out quickly, possibly by a compositor working directly in type. Certainly, the English spellings were uncharacteristic of Crane, and since Copeland and Day had probably complied with his request that they return the manuscripts of the book to him, they were probably

---

4 Crane to Copeland and Day, 29 May 1895, *Letters*, p. 56.

lx

made at the request of Heinemann.

English reviewers of *The Black Riders* were only slightly more gentle in their attentions than were the American reviewers, but there was evidently sufficient demand for the book to warrant the first English impression, Publication 17. Copyright deposit of this third impression of the first edition was made on 13 November 1896, and the book was announced in the *Publishers' Circular,* 14 November 1896. While Crane presented an inscribed copy of this impression to Henry D. Davray in an attempt to persuade him to translate the book for French publication,[5] there is no evidence that he participated in any degree in the preparation of this impression. Instead, the contents of the text of the second impression were left standing and new preliminary matter was machined. Publication 17 collates as follows:

(*Title,* p. [iii]) : THE BLACK RIDERS AND | OTHER LINES BY STE- | PHEN CRANE [three leaf ornaments] | [acorn ornament] | LONDON: WILLIAM HEINEMANN | MDCCCXCVI

(*Printer's imprint and copyright notice,* p. [iv]) : PRINTED BY JOHN WILSON AND SON CAMBRIDGE U.S.A. | *All rights reserved*

(*Dedication,* p. [v]) : TO HAMLIN GARLAND

(*Collation*): (6 x 4 1/4 inches) : [unsigned: $\pi^4$ ($=F_{7-8}$) $x^1$ B—F$^8$ ($-F_{7-8}$) ; 41 leaves, pp. [i-vi] 1-76

(*Contents*) : p. [i], half-title, THE BLACK RIDERS | AND OTHER LINES; p. [ii], *By the same Author* | THE RED BADGE OF COURAGE | [rule] | MAGGIE | A Child of the Streets | [rule] | THE LITTLE REGIMENT | [rule]

---

[5] The volume is dated 11 November 1897 by Crane. This copy is in the Clifton Waller Barrett collection (see Baum, *Crane: An Exhibition,* p. 22). The attempt to provide a French publication of the book during Crane's lifetime failed.

[*Shortly* | *This Edition is limited to Five Hundred copies*; p. [iii], title; p. [iv], printer's imprint and copyright notice; p. [v], dedication; pp. 1-76, text as in second impression.

(*Binding*) : Black leather. Front: [set flush left, printed in gold] THE BLACK RIDERS | AND OTHER | LINES | BY | STEPHEN | CRANE | [orchid design blindstamped]. Spine: [printed in gold] THE | BLACK | RIDERS | STEPHEN | CRANE | HEINEMANN. Blindstamped on the back is a mirror-image of the orchid design on the front. Gatherings of two leaves of book stock are used as binder's leaves and paste-downs at the front and back. The top edges of the pages are gilded.

The changes in the preliminary matter evidently were made in standing type of the second impression. Forms $F_1^r$ to $F_6^v$ (pp. 65-76) were left standing. The half-title was set on the formerly blank $F_8^v$; *"By the same Author"* was set on the formerly blank $F_8^r$; the new title-page was set on the formerly blank $F_7^v$; and additions were made to the printer's imprint on $F_7^r$. The conjugate leaves $F_{7\cdot8}$ were bound as pp. [i-iv], and the dedication page (printed from standing type of the previous impressions) was tipped in as pp. [v-vi]. Naturally, leaves $F_1$, $F_2$ were disjuncted in this process, and they were tipped into their proper place preceding $F_3$.

The second edition of *The Black Riders*, Publication 29, was produced by permission of Small, Maynard and Company in 1905, five years after Crane's death. This edition collates as follows:

(*Title*, p. [iii]): THE BLACK RIDERS AND | OTHER LINES | BY STEPHEN CRANE | PRIVATELY RE-PRINTED | BY COURTESY OF SMALL, MAYNARD & COMPANY | COPYRIGHT, 1905, BY COPELAND & DAY

(*Collation*): (7x5 inches): [unsigned: A—E$^8$]; 40 leaves, pp. [i - iv 1-76].

(*Contents*): pp. [i-ii], blank; p. [iii], title; p. [iv], blank; [poems in the volume headed by numerals I-LXVIII, reference here to the poems is by number in this edition] pp. [1-48] poems *1-48,* one to a page; pp. [49-50], *49;* pp. [51-69], poems *50-68,* one to a page]; pp. [70-76], blank.

(*Typography and paper*): 29 lines (unleaded), 4 3/4 (5 1/4) x 3; 12 pt. Caslon Old Face. Cream laid paper with vertical chainlines 1 3/16 inches apart, with horizontal wirelines, and with a watermark: [in a diamond] D | QUEEN LAID; all edges cut; sheets bulk 7/32".

(*Binding*): Gray boards with 2 5/16 white cloth tape around the spine, extending onto front and back. Front: [a white paper label, 2 x 3, glued 2" from the top] THE BLACK RIDERS AND | OTHER LINES | BY STEPHEN CRANE

Crane corrected proof for the first impression of the first edition, Publication 1. On 2 January 1895, he returned a "proof sheet" to Copeland and Day, stating that he did not care to see corrected proof. On 14 January he asked for more proof, and noted that he would leave for the West at the end of the week. (The trip was actually postponed until about 28 January.) It is improbable that Crane had anything further to do with the preparation of the text of Publication 1, and most unlikely that he participated in any way in the succeeding impressions.

While he was in New York and relatively available until early November, 1896, it is quite probable that the orthographical revisions and the corrections in *61* and in *64* originated from Copeland and Day. Since Crane invariably used American spellings (frequently misspelling) , to have involved him in a task that any editor could have performed would have been to create an unnecessary complication in an otherwise simple affair. And since Publication 17 is but a further impression of the revised impression, Publication 7, his participation in the preparation of this volume is unlikely in the extreme.

The second edition, Publication 29, rests its claim to authority on its association with the successor to the original publisher of the book (Small, Maynard and Company bought *The Black Riders* and sixty other titles at the bankruptcy sale of Copeland and Day in May, 1899). But collation of the edition refutes the claim. H. P. Davis, for whom the volume was published in an edition of 400 copies,[6] attempted to translate into the usual upper- and lower-case convention the completely upper-case volumes sponsored by Copeland and Day. In so doing, he used capitalization to stress heavily personification and anti-deitic patterns. And yet, since the manuscripts were unavailable to him, these casts were probably the result of the editor's conception of the volume.

Publication 32, *The Collected Poems* of 1930, is a reprint of the text that Wilson Follett produced for *The Work of Stephen Crane,* Volume VI, 1926 (Publication 30). These two volumes constitute the two collected editions of Crane's poems. Follett's text is less radical than that of Publication 29, but Follett adopted the Anglicisms of the later impressions of the first edition, modified to a degree the system of punctuation, changed the blocking of several poems, made no attempt to encompass the variant printings of *33, 99* caused by its republication in *War Is Kind,* and tampered with the integrity of *War Is Kind* by including *74* in that section of the collection.

Since the present edition of Crane's poems attempts to present a text that represents the author's final consideration of each poem, Publication 1 has been used as the authoritative edition. (Authority is denied Publications 13, 14, and 27 as

---

6 Williams and Starrett, *Stephen Crane: A Bibliography,* p. 86.

sources of the texts of *The Black Riders*. It is improbable that Elbert Hubbard did more than adapt the presentation of *24* from Publication 1 when presenting it in Publication 13, and it is equally clear that the texts of *9* and *10* in Publication 14 are reprints of the appearances in Publication 1. Since Crane referred Stedman to his books when Stedman asked for a contribution to the *American Anthology*—Publication 27— one may assume that the variants in this publication are editorially inspired.) While the substantive readings in Publication 1 have been presented in the present text of the poems, certain inconsistencies in the accidentals have been modified.

For example, tabulation of the manuscripts of the poems shows that Crane invariably used a colon to introduce quotations. The conformity to the more usual differentiation between the colon and the comma in this respect in Publication 1 has been set to house styling, and therefore this edition of the poetry records the manuscript usage of the colon.

Again, while Crane agreed to the presentation of the volume in capital letters throughout, it has been considered necessary to provide a text in both upper- and lower-case letters. In the five poems for which manuscripts survive, these have been followed. For the remaining poems, the present treatment is extremely conservative. Only when personification of the abstract ("Good Deed" and "Vanity" in *60*, for example) is undeniably intended is the initial letter of a word in the middle of a line capitalized; and only when a monotheistic system is operable within a poem, or when the Judeo-Christian deity is pronounced, is the word "God" so indicated.

Two minor deviations in the treatment of accidentals have been imposed on this edition. The practice of preceding each line of a quotation by opening quotation marks has been dropped, while the roman numerals with which each poem in the volume was identified have been replaced by arabic numerals in italics referring to the List of Poems in this edition.

WAR IS KIND

Publication 24, the first edition, was published by Frederick A. Stokes Company on 20 May 1899.

(*Title*, p. [5]): [all in fancy lettering, within a compartment 6 9/16 x 3 5/8 inches; three lines within a frame 3 1/16 x 2 3/8:] WAR is | KIND by | STEPHEN CRANE | [a stylized lute ornament within a frame 11/16 x 2 3/8] | [three lines within a frame 1 1/8 x 2 3/8:] DRAWINGS | by WILL | BRADLEY | [an empty frame 5/8 x 2 3/8] | [four lines within a frame 1 1/8 x 2 3/8:] NEW YORK | FREDERICK A. | STOKES Company | MDCCCXCIX

(*Copyright notice and printer's imprint*, p. [6]): Copyright 1899, by | Frederick A. Stokes Company | *Arranged and Printed by Will Bradley at the* | *University Press, Cambridge and New York*

(*Collation*): [unsigned: A—B² C—I⁴ J⁸ K—L⁴ M²]; 50 leaves, pp. [1-8] 9-12 [13-14] 15-28 [29-30] 31-36 [37-38] 39-60 [61-62] 63-74 [75-76] 77-96 [97-100]

(*Contents*): pp. [1-4], blank, used as pastedowns and binder's leaves; p. [5], title; p. [6], copyright notice and printer's imprint; pp. [7-8], drawings; [poems in the volume begin with oversize initial letter and remainder of initial word in caps; poems here identified by reference to number in this edition] pp. 9-10, *76* (section title on p. 9: [leaf ornament] WAR IS KIND); pp. 11-12, 15-18, *77*; pp. [13-14], drawings; pp. 19-20, *78;* pp. 21-22, *79;* p. 23, *80;* pp. 24-26, *81;* p. 27, *82;* p. 28, *83;* pp. [29-30], drawings; pp. 31-34, *84;* p. 35, *85;* pp. 36, 39, *86;* pp. [37-38], drawings; p. 40, *87;* p. 41, *88;* p. 42, *89;* p. 43,

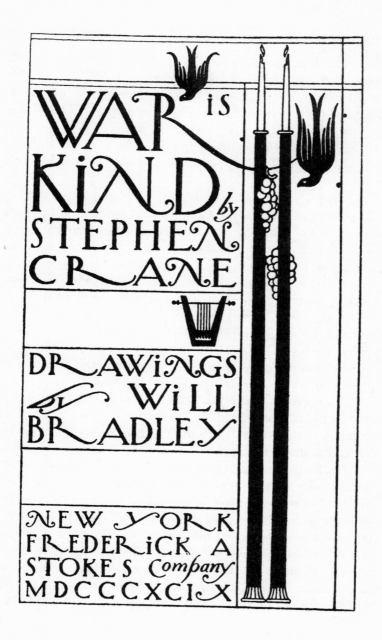

Facsimile of the title page of *War Is Kind* (Publication 24). Reproduced from the copy in the Butler Library of Columbia University.

*90*; p. 44, *91*; p. 45, *92*; pp. 46-49, *93*; pp. 50-53, *94*; pp. 54-55, *95*; p. 56, *96*; p. 57, *97*; p. 58, *98*; p. 59, *99* [=*33*]; p. 60, *100*; pp. [61-62], drawings; pp. 63-64, *101*; pp. 65-66, *102*; pp. 67-74, 77-80, *103* (section title on p. 67: [leaf ornament] INTRIGUE); pp. [75-76], drawings; pp. 81-88, *104*; p. 89, *105*; p. 90, *106*; p. 91, *107*; p. 92, *108*; p. 93, *109;* p. 94, *110;* p. 95, *111*; p. 96, *112*; pp. [97-100], blank, used as pastedown and binder's leaves.

This is the only edition of *War Is Kind* published during Crane's lifetime. But while Crane authorized the publication of the volume, there is no evidence that he even corrected proof for it. Certainly, some of the readings incorporated in Publication 24 are extremely doubtful. Instead, it is probable that he collected many of the published poems, added to these several unpublished poems, and prepared a typescript copy of the text of the volume for submission to the publisher (see pp. xlix-l, above). Thus, many of the poems in *War Is Kind* survive in several states: in manuscript, in fair copy, in corrected proof, in the pages of the periodicals, and in the carbon copy of the typescript submitted to Stokes.

The typescript, as the final stage in which Crane participated, must be considered the authoritative version of *War Is Kind*. (See the Notes to *93* and *103*.) But the problems posed by acknowledging this authority are many. The typescript was prepared hastily; occasionally, Crane recorded in it the readings of earlier states of a poem, and frequently he made careless mistakes in substantive as well as accidental readings. In establishing the text of *War Is Kind*, this typescript has been used as the basic source of the texts of the poems, but inconsistencies within the typescript text of any poem have been resolved, whenever possible, by reference to the authoritative version immediately preceding the typescript on the family tree of the poem. (The typescript is composed of the following

drafts: I; L, M; O; P; R; T; V; X; Y, BB; CC, DD; II;
LL; MM; NN; OO; PP; QQ; RR.)

POSTHUMOUSLY PUBLISHED POEMS

The twenty-two poems in this section were left by Crane
in various stages of completion at his death. They span his
entire poetic career, from his earliest attempts at writing
verse, through his composition of *The Black Riders,* through
his travels to the scenes of battle, to the period shortly before
his death. To have distributed these poems according to their
dates of composition would have disrupted the integrity of the
two published volumes and the published poems that had not
been collected by him. For this reason, while it has been
possible to date these poems to one degree or another, they
have been placed as a group and have been arranged in the
approximate order of composition. In all cases, the text of the
poems in this edition reproduces the texts of the final states in
Crane's draft.

# THE POEMS OF STEPHEN CRANE

# THE BLACK RIDERS AND OTHER LINES

1

Black riders came from the sea.
There was clang and clang of spear and shield,
And clash and clash of hoof and heel,
Wild shouts and the wave of hair
In the rush upon the wind:
Thus the ride of Sin.

2　　Three little birds in a row
　　　　Sat musing.
　　　　A man passed near that place.
　　　　Then did the little birds nudge each other.

　　　　They said: "He thinks he can sing."
　　　　They threw back their heads to laugh.
　　　　With quaint countenances
　　　　They regarded him.
　　　　They were very curious,
　　　　Those three little birds in a row.

3     In the desert
      I saw a creature, naked, bestial,
      Who, squatting upon the ground,
      Held his heart in his hands,
      And ate of it.
      I said: "Is it good, friend?"
      "It is bitter—bitter," he answered;
      "But I like it
      Because it is bitter,
      And because it is my heart."

*4*        Yes, I have a thousand tongues,
And nine and ninety-nine lie.
Though I strive to use the one,
It will make no melody at my will,
But is dead in my mouth.

5    Once there came a man
Who said:
"Range me all men of the world in rows."
And instantly
There was terrific clamor among the people
Against being ranged in rows.
There was a loud quarrel, world-wide.
It endured for ages;
And blood was shed
By those who would not stand in rows,
And by those who pined to stand in rows.
Eventually, the man went to death, weeping.
And those who stayed in bloody scuffle
Knew not the great simplicity.

6     God fashioned the ship of the world carefully.
With the infinite skill of an all-master
Made He the hull and the sails,
Held He the rudder
Ready for adjustment.
Erect stood He, scanning His work proudly.
Then—at fateful time—a wrong called,
And God turned, heeding.
Lo, the ship, at this opportunity, slipped slyly,
Making cunning noiseless travel down the ways.
So that, forever rudderless, it went upon the seas
Going ridiculous voyages,
Making quaint progress,
Turning as with serious purpose
Before stupid winds.
And there were many in the sky
Who laughed at this thing.

7       Mystic shadow, bending near me,
        Who art thou?
        Whence come ye?
        And—tell me—is it fair
        Or is the truth bitter as eaten fire?
        Tell me!
        Fear not that I should quaver,
        For I dare—I dare.
        Then, tell me!

*8*     I looked here;
I looked there;
Nowhere could I see my love.
And—this time—
She was in my heart.
Truly, then, I have no complaint,
For though she be fair and fairer,
She is none so fair as she
In my heart.

9   I stood upon a high place,
And saw, below, many devils
Running, leaping,
And carousing in sin.
One looked up, grinning,
And said: "Comrade! Brother!"

*10*      Should the wide world roll away,
Leaving black terror,
Limitless night,
Nor God, nor man, nor place to stand
Would be to me essential,
If thou and thy white arms were there,
And the fall to doom a long way.

11      In a lonely place,
        I encountered a sage
        Who sat, all still,
        Regarding a newspaper.
        He accosted me:
        "Sir, what is this?"
        Then I saw that I was greater,
        Aye, greater than this sage.
        I answered him at once:
        "Old, old man, it is the wisdom of the age."
        The sage looked upon me with admiration.

12      "And the sins of the fathers shall be visited upon the heads of the children, even unto the third and fourth generation of them that hate me."

Well, then, I hate Thee, unrighteous picture;
Wicked image, I hate Thee;
So, strike with Thy vengeance
The heads of those little men
Who come blindly.
It will be a brave thing.

13       If there is a witness to my little life,
To my tiny throes and struggles,
He sees a fool;
And it is not fine for gods to menace fools.

14      There was crimson clash of war.
Lands turned black and bare;
Women wept;
Babes ran, wondering.
There came one who understood not these things.
He said: "Why is this?"
Whereupon a million strove to answer him.
There was such intricate clamor of tongues,
That still the reason was not.

15        "Tell brave deeds of war."

Then they recounted tales:
"There were stern stands
And bitter runs for glory."

Ah, I think there were braver deeds.

16    Charity, thou art a lie,
A toy of women,
A pleasure of certain men.
In the presence of justice,
Lo, the walls of the temple
Are visible
Through thy form of sudden shadows.

17    There were many who went in huddled procession,
     They knew not whither;
     But, at any rate, success or calamity
     Would attend all in equality.

     There was one who sought a new road.
     He went into direful thickets,
     And ultimately he died thus, alone;
     But they said he had courage.

18     In Heaven,
       Some little blades of grass
       Stood before God.
       "What did you do?"
       Then all save one of the little blades
       Began eagerly to relate
       The merits of their lives.
       This one stayed a small way behind,
       Ashamed.
       Presently, God said:
       "And what did you do?"
       The little blade answered: "Oh, my Lord,
       Memory is bitter to me,
       For, if I did good deeds,
       I know not of them."
       Then God, in all His splendor,
       Arose from His throne.
       "Oh, best little blade of grass!" He said.

19      A god in wrath
        Was beating a man;
        He cuffed him loudly
        With thunderous blows
        That rang and rolled over the earth.
        All people came running.
        The man screamed and struggled,
        And bit madly at the feet of the god.
        The people cried:
        "Ah, what a wicked man!"
        And—
        "Ah, what a redoubtable god!"

20
A learned man came to me once.
He said: "I know the way,—come."
And I was overjoyed at this.
Together we hastened.
Soon, too soon, were we
Where my eyes were useless,
And I knew not the ways of my feet.
I clung to the hand of my friend;
But at last he cried: "I am lost."

21      There was, before me,
Mile upon mile
Of snow, ice, burning sand.
And yet I could look beyond all this,
To a place of infinite beauty;
And I could see the loveliness of her
Who walked in the shade of the trees.
When I gazed,
All was lost
But this place of beauty and her.
When I gazed,
And in my gazing, desired,
Then came again
Mile upon mile,
Of snow, ice, burning sand.

22        Once I saw mountains angry,
And ranged in battle-front.
Against them stood a little man;
Aye, he was no bigger than my finger.
I laughed, and spoke to one near me:
"Will he prevail?"
"Surely," replied this other;
"His grandfathers beat them many times."
Then did I see much virtue in grandfathers,—
At least, for the little man
Who stood against the mountains.

23      Places among the stars,
Soft gardens near the sun,
Keep your distant beauty;
Shed no beams upon my weak heart.
Since she is here
In a place of blackness,
Not your golden days
Nor your silver nights
Can call me to you.
Since she is here
In a place of blackness,
Here I stay and wait.

24     I saw a man pursuing the horizon;
Round and round they sped.
I was disturbed at this;
I accosted the man.
"It is futile," I said,
"You can never—"

"You lie," he cried,
And ran on.

25       Behold, the grave of a wicked man,
And near it, a stern spirit.

There came a drooping maid with violets,
But the spirit grasped her arm.
"No flowers for him," he said.
The maid wept:
"Ah, I loved him."
But the spirit, grim and frowning:
"No flowers for him."

Now, this is it—
If the spirit was just,
Why did the maid weep?

26     There was set before me a mighty hill,
And long days I climbed
Through regions of snow.
When I had before me the summit-view,
It seemed that my labor
Had been to see gardens
Lying at impossible distances.

27    A youth in apparel that glittered
Went to walk in a grim forest.
There he met an assassin
Attired all in garb of old days;
He, scowling through the thickets,
And dagger poised quivering,
Rushed upon the youth.
"Sir," said this latter,
"I am enchanted, believe me,
To die, thus,
In this medieval fashion,
According to the best legends;
Ah, what joy!"
Then took he the wound, smiling,
And died, content.

28     "Truth," said a traveller,
"Is a rock, a mighty fortress;
Often have I been to it,
Even to its highest tower,
From whence the world looks black."

"Truth," said a traveller,
"Is a breath, a wind,
A shadow, a phantom;
Long have I pursued it,
But never have I touched
The hem of its garment."

And I believed the second traveller;
For truth was to me
A breath, a wind,
A shadow, a phantom,
And never had I touched
The hem of its garment.

29   Behold, from the land of the farther suns
     I returned.
     And I was in a reptile-swarming place,
     Peopled, otherwise, with grimaces,
     Shrouded above in black impenetrableness.
     I shrank, loathing,
     Sick with it.
     And I said to him:
     "What is this?"
     He made answer slowly:
     "Spirit, this is a world;
     This was your home."

30      Supposing that I should have the courage
To let a red sword of virtue
Plunge into my heart,
Letting to the weeds of the ground
My sinful blood,
What can you offer me?
A gardened castle?
A flowery kingdom?

What? A hope?
Then hence with your red sword of virtue.

31      Many workmen
        Built a huge ball of masonry
        Upon a mountain-top.
        Then they went to the valley below,
        And turned to behold their work.
        "It is grand," they said;
        They loved the thing.

        Of a sudden, it moved:
        It came upon them swiftly;
        It crushed them all to blood.
        But some had opportunity to squeal.

32    Two or three angels
      Came near to the earth.
      They saw a fat church.
      Little black streams of people
      Came and went in continually.
      And the angels were puzzled
      To know why the people went thus,
      And why they stayed so long within.

33     There was One I met upon the road
       Who looked at me with kind eyes.
       He said: "Show me of your wares."
       And I did,
       Holding forth one.
       He said: "It is a sin."
       Then I held forth another.
       He said: "It is a sin."
       Then I held forth another.
       He said: "It is a sin."
       And so to the end.
       Always He said: "It is a sin."
       At last, I cried out:
       "But I have none other."
       He looked at me
       With kinder eyes.
       "Poor soul," He said.

34  I stood upon a highway,
    And, behold, there came
    Many strange pedlers.
    To me each one made gestures,
    Holding forth little images, saying:
    "This is my pattern of God.
    Now this is the God I prefer."

    But I said: "Hence!
    Leave me with mine own,
    And take you yours away;
    I can't buy of your patterns of God,
    The little gods you may rightly prefer."

35    A man saw a ball of gold in the sky;
      He climbed for it,
      And eventually he achieved it—
      It was clay.

      Now this is the strange part:
      When the man went to the earth
      And looked again,
      Lo, there was the ball of gold.
      Now this is the strange part:
      It was a ball of gold.
      Aye, by the heavens, it was a ball of gold.

36    I met a seer.
He held in his hands
The book of wisdom.
"Sir," I addressed him,
"Let me read."
"Child—" he began.
"Sir," I said,
"Think not that I am a child,
For already I know much
Of that which you hold.
Aye, much."

He smiled.
Then he opened the book
And held it before me.—
Strange that I should have grown so suddenly blind.

37      On the horizon the peaks assembled;
And as I looked,
The march of the mountains began.
As they marched, they sang:
"Aye! We come! We come!"

*38*      The ocean said to me once:
"Look!
Yonder on the shore
Is a woman, weeping.
I have watched her.
Go you and tell her this,—
Her lover I have laid
In cool green hall.
There is wealth of golden sand
And pillars, coral-red;
Two white fish stand guard at his bier.

"Tell her this
And more,—
That the king of the seas
Weeps too, old, helpless man.
The bustling fates
Heap his hands with corpses
Until he stands like a child
With surplus of toys."

39    The livid lightnings flashed in the clouds;
The leaden thunders crashed.
A worshipper raised his arm.
"Hearken! Hearken! The voice of God!"

"Not so," said a man.
"The voice of God whispers in the heart
So softly
That the soul pauses,
Making no noise,
And strives for these melodies,
Distant, sighing, like faintest breath,
And all the being is still to hear."

*40*     And you love me?

I love you.

You are, then, cold coward.

Aye; but, beloved,
When I strive to come to you,
Man's opinions, a thousand thickets,
My interwoven existence,
My life,
Caught in the stubble of the world
Like a tender veil,—
This stays me.
No strange move can I make
Without noise of tearing.
I dare not.

If love loves,
There is no world
Nor word.
All is lost
Save thought of love
And place to dream.
You love me?

I love you.

You are, then, cold coward.

Aye; but, beloved—

*41*      Love walked alone.
The rocks cut her tender feet,
And the brambles tore her fair limbs.
There came a companion to her,
But, alas, he was no help,
For his name was Heart's Pain.

42      I walked in a desert.
And I cried:
"Ah, God, take me from this place!"
A voice said: "It is no desert."
I cried: "Well, but—
The sand, the heat, the vacant horizon."
A voice said: "It is no desert."

43 There came whisperings in the winds:
"Good-bye! Good-bye!"
Little voices called in the darkness:
"Good-bye! Good-bye!"
Then I stretched forth my arms.
"No— No—"
There came whisperings in the wind:
"Good-bye! Good-bye!"
Little voices called in the darkness:
"Good-bye! Good-bye!"

44    I was in the darkness;
      I could not see my words
      Nor the wishes of my heart.
      Then suddenly there was a great light—

      "Let me into the darkness again."

45      Tradition, thou art for suckling children,
Thou art the enlivening milk for babes;
But no meat for men is in thee.
Then—
But, alas, we all are babes.

*46*       Many red devils ran from my heart
And out upon the page.
They were so tiny
The pen could mash them.
And many struggled in the ink.
It was strange
To write in this red muck
Of things from my heart.

47 "Think as I think," said a man,
"Or you are abominably wicked,
You are a toad."

And after I had thought of it,
I said: "I will, then, be a toad."

48    Once there was a man,—
Oh, so wise!
In all drink
He detected the bitter,
And in all touch
He found the sting.
At last he cried thus:
"There is nothing,—
No life,
No joy,
No pain,—
There is nothing save opinion,
And opinion be damned."

49 I stood musing in a black world,
Not knowing where to direct my feet.
And I saw the quick stream of men
Pouring ceaselessly,
Filled with eager faces,
A torrent of desire.
I called to them:
"Where do you go? What do you see?"
A thousand voices called to me.
A thousand fingers pointed.
"Look! Look! There!"

I know not of it.
But, lo! in the far sky shone a radiance
Ineffable, divine,—
A vision painted upon a pall;
And sometimes it was,
And sometimes it was not.
I hesitated.
Then from the stream
Came roaring voices,
Impatient:
"Look! Look! There!"

So again I saw,
And leaped, unhesitant,
And struggled and fumed
With outspread clutching fingers.
The hard hills tore my flesh;
The ways bit my feet.
At last I looked again.
No radiance in the far sky,
Ineffable, divine,
No vision painted upon a pall;
And always my eyes ached for the light.
Then I cried in despair:
"I see nothing! Oh, where do I go?"
The torrent turned again its faces:
"Look! Look! There!"

And at the blindness of my spirit
They screamed:
"Fool! Fool! Fool!"

*50*      You say you are holy,
And that
Because I have not seen you sin.
Aye, but there are those
Who see you sin, my friend.

51      A man went before a strange god,—
The god of many men, sadly wise.
And the deity thundered loudly,
Fat with rage, and puffing:
"Kneel, mortal, and cringe
And grovel and do homage
To my particularly sublime majesty."

                The man fled.

Then the man went to another god,—
The god of his inner thoughts.
And this one looked at him
With soft eyes
Lit with infinite comprehension,
And said: "My poor child!"

52      Why do you strive for greatness, fool?
Go pluck a bough and wear it.
It is as sufficing.

My Lord, there are certain barbarians
Who tilt their noses
As if the stars were flowers,
And thy servant is lost among their shoe-buckles.
Fain would I have mine eyes even with their eyes.

Fool, go pluck a bough and wear it.

53                                    I

    Blustering god,
    Stamping across the sky
    With loud swagger,
    I fear you not.
    No, though from your highest heaven
    You plunge your spear at my heart,
    I fear you not.
    No, not if the blow
    Is as the lightning blasting a tree,
    I fear you not, puffing braggart.

II

    If thou can see into my heart
    That I fear thee not,
    Thou wilt see why I fear thee not,
    And why it is right.
    So threaten not, thou, with thy bloody spears,
    Else thy sublime ears shall hear curses.

III

    Withal, there is one whom I fear;
    I fear to see grief upon that face.
    Perchance, friend, he is not your god;
    If so, spit upon him.
    By it you will do no profanity.
    But I—
    Ah, sooner would I die
    Than see tears in those eyes of my soul.

57

54      "It was wrong to do this," said the angel.
"You should live like a flower,
Holding malice like a puppy,
Waging war like a lambkin."

"Not so," quoth the man
Who had no fear of spirits;
"It is only wrong for angels
Who can live like the flowers,
Holding malice like the puppies,
Waging war like the lambkins."

55 A man toiled on a burning road,
   Never resting.
   Once he saw a fat, stupid ass
   Grinning at him from a green place.
   The man cried out in rage:
   "Ah! do not deride me, fool!
   I know you—
   All day stuffing your belly,
   Burying your heart
   In grass and tender sprouts:
   It will not suffice you."
   But the ass only grinned at him from the green place.

56  A man feared that he might find an assassin;
    Another that he might find a victim.
    One was more wise than the other.

57  With eye and with gesture
    You say you are holy.
    I say you lie;
    For I did see you
    Draw away your coats
    From the sin upon the hands
    Of a little child.
    Liar!

58       The sage lectured brilliantly.
Before him, two images:
"Now this one is a devil,
And this one is me."
He turned away.
Then a cunning pupil
Changed the positions.
Turned the sage again:
"Now this one is a devil,
And this one is me."
The pupils sat, all grinning,
And rejoiced in the game.
But the sage was a sage.

59 Walking in the sky,
  A man in strange black garb
  Encountered a radiant form.
  Then his steps were eager;
  Bowed he devoutly.
  "My Lord," said he.
  But the spirit knew him not.

60 Upon the road of my life,
Passed me many fair creatures,
Clothed all in white, and radiant.
To one, finally, I made speech:
"Who art thou?"
But she, like the others,
Kept cowled her face,
And answered in haste, anxiously:
"I am Good Deed, forsooth;
You have often seen me."
"Not uncowled," I made reply.
And with rash and strong hand,
Though she resisted,
I drew away the veil
And gazed at the features of Vanity.
She, shamefaced, went on;
And after I had mused a time,
I said of myself:
     "Fool!"

*61*

### I

There was a man and a woman
Who sinned.
Then did the man heap the punishment
All upon the head of her,
And went away gayly.

### II

There was a man and a woman
Who sinned.
And the man stood with her.
As upon her head, so upon his,
Fell blow and blow,
And all people screaming: "Fool!"
He was a brave heart.

### III

He was a brave heart.
Would you speak with him, friend?
Well, he is dead,
And there went your opportunity.
Let it be your grief
That he is dead
And your opportunity gone;
For, in that, you were a coward.

62    There was a man who lived a life of fire.
Even upon the fabric of time,
Where purple becomes orange
And orange purple,
This life glowed,
A dire red stain, indelible;
Yet when he was dead,
He saw that he had not lived.

63      There was a great cathedral.
To solemn songs,
A white procession
Moved toward the altar.
The chief man there
Was erect, and bore himself proudly.
Yet some could see him cringe,
As in a place of danger,
Throwing frightened glances into the air,
A-start at threatening faces of the past.

64      Friend, your white beard sweeps the ground.
Why do you stand, expectant?
Do you hope to see it
In one of your withered days?
With your old eyes
Do you hope to see
The triumphal march of justice?
Do not wait, friend!
Take your white beard
And your old eyes
To more tender lands.

65    Once, I knew a fine song,
      —It is true, believe me,—
      It was all of birds,
      And I held them in a basket;
      When I opened the wicket,
      Heavens! they all flew away.
      I cried: "Come back little thoughts!"
      But they only laughed.
      They flew on
      Until they were as sand
      Thrown between me and the sky.

66    If I should cast off this tattered coat,
      And go free into the mighty sky;
      If I should find nothing there
      But a vast blue,
      Echoless, ignorant,—
      What then?

67      God lay dead in Heaven;
Angels sang the hymn of the end;
Purple winds went moaning,
Their wings drip-dripping
With blood
That fell upon the earth.
It, groaning thing,
Turned black and sank.
Then from the far caverns
Of dead sins
Came monsters, livid with desire.
They fought,
Wrangled over the world,
A morsel.
But of all sadness this was sad,—
A woman's arms tried to shield
The head of a sleeping man
From the jaws of the final beast.

68    A spirit sped
      Through spaces of night;
      And as he sped, he called:
      "God! God!"
      He went through valleys
      Of black death-slime,
      Ever calling:
      "God! God!"
      Their echoes
      From crevice and cavern
      Mocked him:
      "God! God! God!"
      Fleetly into the plains of space
      He went, ever calling:
      "God! God!"
      Eventually, then, he screamed,
      Mad in denial:
      "Ah, there is no God!"
      A swift hand,
      A sword from the sky,
      Smote him,
      And he was dead.

*UNCOLLECTED POEMS*

## "LEGENDS"

*69*

### I

A man builded a bugle for the storms to blow.
The focussed winds hurled him afar.
He said that the instrument was a failure.

*70*

### II

When the suicide arrived at the sky, the people
    there asked him: "Why?"
He replied: "Because no one admired me."

*71*

### III

A man said: "Thou tree!"
The tree answered with the same scorn: "Thou man!
Thou art greater than I only in thy possibilities."

*72*

### IV

A warrior stood upon a peak and defied the stars.
A little magpie, happening there, desired the
    soldier's plume, and so plucked it.

*73*

### V

The wind that waves the blossoms sang, sang, sang
    from age to age.
The flowers were made curious by this joy.
"Oh, wind," they said, "why sing you at your
    labour, while we, pink beneficiaries, sing
    not, but idle, idle, idle from age to age?"

75

74      When a people reach the top of a hill
Then does God lean toward them,
Shortens tongues, lengthens arms.
A vision of their dead comes to the weak.
    The moon shall not be too old
    Before the new battalions rise
      —Blue battalions—
    The moon shall not be too old
    When the children of change shall fall
    Before the new battalions
      —The blue battalions—

Mistakes and virtues will be trampled deep
A church and a thief shall fall together
A sword will come at the bidding of the eyeless,
The God-led, turning only to beckon.
    Swinging a creed like a censer
    At the head of the new battalions
      —Blue battalions—
    March the tools of nature's impulse
    Men born of wrong, men born of right
    Men of the new battalions
      —The blue battalions—

The clang of swords is Thy wisdom
The wounded make gestures like Thy Son's
The feet of mad horses is one part,
—Aye, another is the hand of a mother on the brow of a son.
    Then swift as they charge through a shadow,
    The men of the new battalions
        —Blue battalions—
    God lead them high. God lead them far
    Lead them far, lead them high
    These new battalions
        —The blue battalions—

75     Rumbling, buzzing, turning, whirling Wheels,
Dizzy Wheels!
Wheels!

*WAR IS KIND*

76 Do not weep, maiden, for war is kind.
Because your lover threw wild hands toward the sky
And the affrighted steed ran on alone,
Do not weep.
War is kind.

  Hoarse, booming drums of the regiment,
  Little souls who thirst for fight,
  These men were born to drill and die.
  The unexplained glory flies above them,
  Great is the Battle-God, great, and his Kingdom—
  A field where a thousand corpses lie.

Do not weep, babe, for war is kind.
Because your father tumbled in the yellow trenches,
Raged at his breast, gulped and died,
Do not weep.
War is kind.

  Swift blazing flag of the regiment,
  Eagle with crest of red and gold,
  These men were born to drill and die.
  Point for them the virtue of slaughter,
  Make plain to them the excellence of killing
  And a field where a thousand corpses lie.

Mother whose heart hung humble as a button
On the bright splendid shroud of your son,
Do not weep.
War is kind.

81

77
"What says the sea, little shell?
What says the sea?
Long has our brother been silent to us,
Kept his message for the ships,
Awkward ships, stupid ships."

"The sea bids you mourn, oh, pines,
Sing low in the moonlight.
He sends tale of the land of doom,
Of place where endless falls
A rain of women's tears,
And men in grey robes—
Men in grey robes—
Chant the unknown pain."

"What says the sea, little shell?
What says the sea?
Long has our brother been silent to us,
Kept his message for the ships,
Puny ships, silly ships."

"The sea bids you teach, oh, pines,
Sing low in the moonlight,
Teach the gold of patience,
Cry gospel of gentle hands,
Cry a brotherhood of hearts.
The sea bids you teach, oh, pines."

"And where is the reward, little shell?
What says the sea?
Long has our brother been silent to us,
Kept his message for the ships,
Puny ships, silly ships."

"No word says the sea, oh, pines,
No word says the sea.
Long will your brother be silent to you,
Keep his message for the ships,
Oh, puny pines, silly pines."

*78*  To the maiden
     The sea was blue meadow
     Alive with little froth-people
     Singing.

     To the sailor, wrecked,
     The sea was dead grey walls
     Superlative in vacancy
     Upon which nevertheless at fateful time
     Was written
     The grim hatred of nature.

79  A little ink more or less!
  It surely can't matter?
  Even the sky and the opulent sea,
  The plains and the hills, aloof,
  Hear the uproar of all these books.
  But it is only a little ink more or less.

  What?
  You define me God with these trinkets?
  Can my misery meal on an ordered walking
  Of surpliced numbskulls?
  And a fanfare of lights?
  Or even upon the measured pulpitings
  Of the familiar false and true?
  Is this God?
  Where, then, is hell?
  Show me some bastard mushroom
  Sprung from a pollution of blood.
  It is better.

  Where is God?

80       "Have you ever made a just man?"
"Oh, I have made three," answered God,
"But two of them are dead
And the third—
Listen! Listen!
And you will hear the third of his defeat."

81    I explain the silvered passing of a ship at night,
The sweep of each sad lost wave
The dwindling boom of the steel thing's striving
The little cry of a man to a man
A shadow falling across the greyer night
And the sinking of the small star.

Then the waste, the far waste of waters
And the soft lashing of black waves
For long and in loneliness.

Remember, thou, O ship of love
Thou leavest a far waste of waters
And the soft lashing of black waves
For long and in loneliness.

82    "I have heard the sunset song of the birches
      A white melody in the silence
      I have seen a quarrel of the pines.
      At nightfall
      The little grasses have rushed by me
      With the wind men.
      These things have I lived," quoth the maniac,
      "Possessing only eyes and ears.
      But, you—
      You don green spectacles before you look at roses."

83     Fast rode the knight
With spurs, hot and reeking
Ever waving an eager sword.
    "To save my lady!"
Fast rode the knight
And leaped from saddle to war.
Men of steel flickered and gleamed
Like riot of silver lights
And the gold of the knight's good banner
Still waved on a castle wall.

   \*    \*    \*    \*    \*    \*    \*    \*    \*    \*    \*

A horse
Blowing, staggering, bloody thing
Forgotten at foot of castle wall.
A horse
Dead at foot of castle wall.

84    Forth went the candid man
And spoke freely to the wind—
When he looked about him he was in a far strange
    country.

Forth went the candid man
And spoke freely to the stars—
Yellow light tore sight from his eyes.

"My good fool," said a learned bystander,
"Your operations are mad."

"You are too candid," cried the candid man
And when his stick left the head of the learned
    bystander
It was two sticks.

85      You tell me this is God?
        I tell you this is a printed list,
        A burning candle and an ass.

86      On the desert
A silence from the moon's deepest valley.
Fire-rays fall athwart the robes
Of hooded men, squat and dumb.
Before them, a woman
Moves to the blowing of shrill whistles
And distant-thunder of drums
While slow things, sinuous, dull with terrible
     color
Sleepily fondle her body
Or move at her will, swishing stealthily over the
     sand.
The snakes whisper softly;
The whispering, whispering snakes
Dreaming and swaying and staring
But always whispering, softly whispering.
The wind streams from the lone reaches
Of Arabia, solemn with night,
And the wild fire makes shimmer of blood
Over the robes of the hooded men
Squat and dumb.
Bands of moving bronze, emerald, yellow
Circle the throat and the arms of her
And over the sands serpents move warily
Slow, menacing and submissive,
Swinging to the whistles and drums,
The whispering, whispering snakes,
Dreaming and swaying and staring
But always whispering, softly whispering.
The dignity of the accurséd;
The glory of slavery, despair, death
Is in the dance of the whispering snakes.

87  A newspaper is a collection of half-injustices
    Which, bawled by boys from mile to mile,
    Spreads its curious opinion
    To a million merciful and sneering men,
    While families cuddle the joys of the fireside
    When spurred by tale of dire lone agony.
    A newspaper is a court
    Where every one is kindly and unfairly tried
    By a squalor of honest men.
    A newspaper is a market
    Where wisdom sells its freedom
    And melons are crowned by the crowd.
    A newspaper is a game
    Where his error scores the player victory
    While another's skill wins death.
    A newspaper is a symbol;
    It is fetless life's chronicle,
    A collection of loud tales
    Concentrating eternal stupidities,
    That in remote ages lived unhaltered,
    Roaming through a fenceless world.

88      The wayfarer
Perceiving the pathway to truth
Was struck with astonishment.
It was thickly grown with weeds.
"Ha," he said,
"I see that none has passed here
In a long time."
Later he saw that each weed
Was a singular knife.
"Well," he mumbled at last,
"Doubtless there are other roads."

89    A slant of sun on dull brown walls
      A forgotten sky of bashful blue.
      Toward God a mighty hymn
      A song of collisions and cries
      Rumbling wheels, hoof-beats, bells,
      Welcomes, farewells, love-calls, final moans,
      Voices of joy, idiocy, warning, despair,
      The unknown appeals of brutes,
      The chanting of flowers
      The screams of cut trees,
      The senseless babble of hens and wise men—
      A cluttered incoherency that says at the stars:
      "Oh, God, save us."

90    Once, a man, clambering to the house-tops,
      Appealed to the heavens.
      With strong voice he called to the deaf spheres;
      A warrior's shout he raised to the suns.
      Lo, at last, there was a dot on the clouds,
      And—at last and at last—
      —God—the sky was filled with armies.

91     There was a man with tongue of wood
       Who essayed to sing,
       And in truth it was lamentable
       But there was one who heard
       The clip-clapper of this tongue of wood
       And knew what the man
       Wished to sing,
       And with that the singer was content.

92    The successful man has thrust himself
Through the water of the years,
Reeking wet with mistakes,
Bloody mistakes;
Slimed with victories over the lesser
A figure thankful on the shore of money.
Then, with the bones of fools
He buys silken banners
Limned with his triumphant face,
With the skins of wise men
He buys the trivial bows of all.
Flesh painted with marrow
Contributes a coverlet
A coverlet for his contented slumber
In guiltless ignorance, in ignorant guilt
He delivers his secrets to the riven multitude.
     "Thus I defended: Thus I wrought."
Complacent, smiling
He stands heavily on the dead.
Erect on a pillar of skulls
He declaims his trampling of babes;
Smirking, fat, dripping
He makes his speech in guiltless ignorance,
Innocence.

93   In the night
Grey, heavy clouds muffled the valleys,
And the peaks looked toward God, alone.
        "Oh, Master that movest the wind with a finger,
        Humble, idle, futile peaks are we.
        Grant that we may run swiftly across the world
        To huddle in worship at Thy feet."

In the morning
A noise of men at work came the clear blue miles
And the little black cities were apparent.
        "Oh, Master that knowest the meaning of rain-drops,
        Humble, idle, futile peaks are we.
        Give voice to us, we pray, O Lord,
        That we may sing Thy goodness to the sun."

In the evening
The far valleys were sprinkled with tiny lights.
        "Oh, Master,
        Thou who knowest the value of kings and birds,
        Thou hast made us humble, idle, futile peaks.
        Thou only needest eternal patience;
        We bow to Thy wisdom, O Lord—
        Humble, idle, futile peaks."

In the night
Grey, heavy clouds muffled the valleys
And the peaks looked toward God, alone.

99

94      The chatter of a death-demon from a tree-top.

Blood—blood and torn grass—
Had marked the rise of his agony—
This lone hunter.
The grey-green woods impassive
Had watched the threshing of his limbs.

A canoe with flashing paddle
A girl with soft searching eyes,
A call: "John!"

\*   \*   \*   \*   \*   \*   \*   \*   \*

Come, arise, hunter!
Can you not hear?

The chatter of a death-demon from a tree-top.

95      The impact of a dollar upon the heart
Smiles warm red light
Sweeping from the hearth rosily upon the white table,
With the hanging cool velvet shadows
Moving softly upon the door.

The impact of a million dollars
Is a crash of flunkeys
And yawning emblems of Persia
Cheeked against oak, France and a sabre,
The outcry of old beauty
Whored by pimping merchants
To submission before wine and chatter.
Silly rich peasants stamp the carpets of men,
Dead men who dreamed fragrance and light
Into their woof, their lives;
The rug of an honest bear
Under the foot of a cryptic slave
Who speaks always of baubles,
Forgetting place, multitude, work and state,
Champing and mouthing of hats
Making ratful squeak of hats,
Hats.

96      A man said to the universe:
"Sir, I exist!"
"However," replied the universe,
"The fact has not created in me
A sense of obligation."

97    When the prophet, a complacent fat man,
      Arrived at the mountain-top
      He cried: "Woe to my knowledge!
      I intended to see good white lands
      And bad black lands—
      But the scene is grey."

98     There was a land where lived no violets.
A traveller at once demanded: "Why?"
The people told him:
"Once the violets of this place spoke thus:
'Until some woman freely gives her lover
To another woman
We will fight in bloody scuffle.' "
Sadly the people added:
"There are no violets here."

99       [See *33* in *The Black Riders and Other Lines.*]

100      Aye, workman, make me a dream
A dream for my love.
Cunningly weave sunlight,
Breezes and flowers.
Let it be of the cloth of meadows.
And—good workman—
And let there be a man walking thereon.

101    Each small gleam was a voice
—A lantern voice—
In little songs of carmine, violet, green, gold.
A chorus of colors came over the water;
The wondrous leaf shadow no longer wavered,
No pines crooned on the hills
The blue night was elsewhere a silence
When the chorus of colors came over the water,
Little songs of carmine, violet, green, gold.

Small glowing pebbles
Thrown on the dark plane of evening
Sing good ballads of God
And eternity, with soul's rest.
Little priests, little holy fathers
None can doubt the truth of your hymning
When the marvellous chorus comes over the water
Songs of carmine, violet, green, gold.

*102*      The trees in the garden rained flowers.
Children ran there joyously.
They gathered the flowers
Each to himself.
Now there were some
Who gathered great heaps—
—Having opportunity and skill—
Until, behold, only chance blossoms
Remained for the feeble.
Then a little spindling tutor
Ran importantly to the father, crying:
"Pray, come hither!
See this unjust thing in your garden!"
But when the father had surveyed,
He admonished the tutor:
"Not so, small sage!
This thing is just.
For, look you,
Are not they who possess the flowers
Stronger, bolder, shrewder
Than they who have none?
Why should the strong—
—The beautiful strong—
Why should they not have the flowers?"

Upon reflection, the tutor bowed to the ground.
"My Lord," he said,
"The stars are misplaced
By this towering wisdom."

## "INTRIGUE"

*103*    Thou art my love
And thou art the peace of sundown
When the blue shadows soothe
And the grasses and the leaves sleep
5 To the song of the little brooks
Woe is me.

Thou art my love
And thou art a storm
That breaks black in the sky
10 And, sweeping headlong,
Drenches and cowers each tree
And at the panting end
There is no sound
Save the melancholy cry of a single owl
15 Woe is me!

Thou art my love
And thou art a tinsel thing
And I in my play
Broke thee easily
20 And from the little fragments
Arose my long sorrow
Woe is me

Thou art my love
And thou art a weary violet
25 Drooping from sun-caresses.
Answering mine carelessly
Woe is me.

Thou art my love
And thou art the ashes of other men's love
30 And I bury my face in these ashes
And I love them
Woe is me

Thou art my love
And thou art the beard
35 On another man's face
Woe is me.

Thou art my love
And thou art a temple
And in this temple is an altar
40 And on this altar is my heart
Woe is me.

Thou art my love
And thou art a wretch.
Let these sacred love-lies choke thee
45 For I am come to where I know your lies as truth
And your truth as lies
Woe is me.

111

Thou art my love
And thou art a priestess
50 And in thy hand is a bloody dagger
And my doom comes to me surely
Woe is me.

Thou art my love
And thou art a skull with ruby eyes
55 And I love thee
Woe is me.

Thou art my love
And I doubt thee
And if peace came with thy murder
60 Then would I murder.
Woe is me.

Thou art my love
And thou art death
Aye, thou art death
65 Black and yet black
But I love thee
I love thee
Woe, welcome woe, to me.

104       Love forgive me if I wish you grief
         For in your grief
         You huddle to my breast
         And for it
5 Would I pay the price of your grief

         You walk among men
         And all men do not surrender
         And this I understand
         That love reaches his hand
10 In mercy to me.

         He had your picture in his room
         A scurvy traitor picture
         And he smiled
         —Merely a fat complacence
15 Of men who know fine women—
         And thus I divided with him
         A part of my love

         Fool, not to know that thy little shoe
         Can make men weep!
20 —Some men weep.
         I weep and I gnash
         And I love the little shoe
         The little, little shoe.

God give me medals
God give me loud honors
That I may strut before you, sweetheart
And be worthy of—
—The love I bear you.

Now let me crunch you
With full weight of affrighted love
I doubted you
—I doubted you—
And in this short doubting
My love grew like a genie
For my further undoing.

Beware of my friends
Be not in speech too civil
For in all courtesy
My weak heart sees spectres,
Mists of desires
Arising from the lips of my chosen
Be not civil.

The flower I gave thee once
Was incident to a stride
A detail of a gesture
But search those pale petals
And see engraven thereon
A record of my intention

114

105      Ah, God, the way your little finger moved
As you thrust a bare arm backward
And made play with your hair
And a comb a silly gilt comb
Ah, God—that I should suffer
Because of the way a little finger moved.

106      Once I saw thee idly rocking
—Idly rocking—
And chattering girlishly to other girls,
Bell-voiced, happy,
Careless with the stout heart of unscarred womanhood
And life to thee was all light melody.
I thought of the great storms of love as I know it
Torn, miserable and ashamed of my open sorrow,
I thought of the thunders that lived in my head
And I wish to be an ogre
And hale and haul my beloved to a castle
And there use the happy cruel one cruelly
And make her mourn with my mourning

107      Tell me why, behind thee,
I see always the shadow of another lover?
Is it real
Or is this the thrice-damned memory of a better
     happiness?
Plague on him if he be dead
Plague on him if he be alive
A swinish numbskull
To intrude his shade
Always between me and my peace

108      And yet I have seen thee happy with me.
I am no fool
To poll stupidly into iron.
I have heard your quick breaths
And seen your arms writhe toward me;
At those times
—God help us—
I was impelled to be a grand knight
And swagger and snap my fingers,
And explain my mind finely.
Oh, lost sweetheart,
I would that I had not been a grand knight.
I said: "Sweetheart."
Thou said'st: "Sweetheart."
And we preserved an admirable mimicry
Without heeding the drip of the blood
From my heart.

109     I heard thee laugh,
        And in this merriment
        I defined the measure of my pain;
        I knew that I was alone,
        Alone with love,
        Poor shivering love,
        And he, little sprite,
        Came to watch with me,
        And at midnight
        We were like two creatures by a dead camp-fire.

*110*
I wonder if sometimes in the dusk,
When the brave lights that gild thy evenings
Have not yet been touched with flame,
I wonder if sometimes in the dusk
Thou rememberest a time,
A time when thou loved me
And our love was to thee all?
Is the memory rubbish now?
An old gown
Worn in an age of other fashions?
Woe is me, oh, lost one,
For that love is now to me
A supernal dream,
White, white, white with many suns.

111      Love met me at noonday,
—Reckless imp,
To leave his shaded nights
And brave the glare,—
And I saw him then plainly
For a bungler,
A stupid, simpering, eyeless bungler,
Breaking the hearts of brave people
As the snivelling idiot-boy cracks his bowl,
And I cursed him,
Cursed him to and fro, back and forth,
Into all the silly mazes of his mind,
But in the end
He laughed and pointed to my breast,
Where a heart still beat for thee, beloved.

*112*     I have seen thy face aflame
For love of me,
Thy fair arms go mad,
Thy lips tremble and mutter and rave.
And—surely—
This should leave a man content?
Thou lovest not me now,
But thou didst love me,
And in loving me once
Thou gavest me an eternal privilege,
For I can think of thee.

*POSTHUMOUSLY PUBLISHED POEMS*

113        A man adrift on a slim spar
A horizon smaller than the rim of a bottle
Tented waves rearing lashy dark points
The near whine of froth in circles.
                  God is cold.

The incessant raise and swing of the sea
And growl after growl of crest
The sinkings, green, seething, endless
The upheaval half-completed.
                  God is cold.

The seas are in the hollow of The Hand;
Oceans may be turned to a spray
Raining down through the stars
Because of a gesture of pity toward a babe.
Oceans may become grey ashes,
Die with a long moan and a roar
Amid the tumult of the fishes
And the cries of the ships,
Because The Hand beckons the mice.

A horizon smaller than a doomed assassin's cap,
Inky, surging tumults
A reeling, drunken sky and no sky
A pale hand sliding from a polished spar.
                  God is cold.

The puff of a coat imprisoning air:
A face kissing the water-death
A weary slow sway of a lost hand
And the sea, the moving sea, the sea.
                  God is cold.

*114*     Chant you loud of punishments,
Of the twisting of the heart's poor strings
Of the crash of the lightning's fierce revenge.

Then sing I of the supple-souled men
And the strong strong gods
That shall meet in times hereafter
And the amaze of the gods
At the strength of the men.
—The strong, strong gods—
—And the supple-souled men—

115  A naked woman and a dead dwarf;
    Wealth and indifference.
    Poor dwarf!
    Reigning with foolish kings
    And dying mid bells and wine
    Ending with a desperate comic palaver
    While before thee and after thee
    Endures the eternal clown—
    —The eternal clown—
    A naked woman.

*116*    Little birds of the night
Aye, they have much to tell
Perching there in rows
Blinking at me with their serious eyes
Recounting of flowers they have seen and loved
Of meadows and groves of the distance
And pale sands at the foot of the sea
And breezes that fly in the leaves
They are vast in experience
These little birds that come in the night

117      Unwind my riddle.
Cruel as hawks the hours fly;
Wounded men seldom come home to die;
The hard waves see an arm flung high;
Scorn hits strong because of a lie;
Yet there exists a mystic tie.
Unwind my riddle.

118    Ah, haggard purse, why ope thy mouth
Like a greedy urchin
I have naught wherewith to feed thee
Thy wan checks have ne'er been puffed
Thou knowest not the fill of pride
Why then gape at me
In fashion of a wronged one
Thou do smilest wanly
And reproachest me with thine empty stomach
Thou knowest I'd sell my steps to the grave
If t'were but honestie
Ha, leer not so,
Name me no names of wrongs committed with thee
No ghost can lay hand on thee and me
We've been too thin to do sin
What, liar? When thou was filled of gold, didst I ri
And give thee no time to eat?
No, thou brown devil, thou art stuffed now with lies as
    with wealth,
The one gone to let in the other.

*119*  One came from the skies
—They said—
And with a band he bound them
A man and a woman.
Now to the man
The band was gold
And to another, iron
And to the woman, iron.
But this second man,
He took his opinion and went away
But, by heavens,
He was none too wise.

120    A god came to a man
And said to him thus:
"I have an apple
It is a glorious apple
Aye, I swear by my ancestors
Of the eternities before this eternity
It is an apple that is from
The inner thoughts of heaven's greatest.

"And this I will hang here
And then I will adjust thee here
Thus—you may reach it.
And you must stifle your nostrils
And control your hands
And your eyes
And sit for sixty years
But,—leave be the apple."

The man answered in this wise:
"Oh, most interesting God
What folly is this?
Behold, thou hast moulded my desires
Even as thou hast moulded the apple.

"How, then?
Can I conquer my life
Which is thou?
My desires?
Look you, foolish god
If I thrust behind me
Sixty white years
I am a greater god than God
And, then, complacent splendor,
Thou wilt see that the golden angels
That sing pink hymns
Around thy throne-top
Will be lower than my feet."

121   There is a grey thing that lives in the tree-tops
      None know the horror of its sight
      Save those who meet death in the wilderness
      But one is enabled to see
      To see branches move at its passing
      To hear at times the wail of black laughter
      And to come often upon mystic places
      Places where the thing has just been.

122       If you would seek a friend among men
         Remember: they are crying their wares.
       If you would ask of heaven of men
         Remember: they are crying their wares
       If you seek the welfare of men
         Remember: they are crying their wares
       If you would bestow a curse upon men
         Remember: they are crying their wares
           Crying their wares
           Crying their wares
       If you seek the attention of men
       Remember:
       Help them or hinder them as they cry their wares.

123    A lad and a maid at a curve in the stream
       And a shine of soft silken waters
       Where the moon-beams fall through a hemlock's boughs
       Oh, night dismal, night glorious.

       A lad and a maid at the rail of a bridge
       With two shadows adrift on the water
       And the wind sings low in the grass on the shore
       Oh, night dismal, night glorious.

       A lad and a maid in a canoe,
       And a paddle making silver turmoil

124    A soldier, young in years, young in ambitions
Alive as no grey-beard is alive
Laid his heart and his hopes before duty
And went staunchly into the tempest of war.
There did the bitter red winds of battle
Swirl 'gainst his youth, beat upon his ambitions,
Drink his cool clear blood of manhood
Until at coming forth time
He was alive merely as the greybeard is alive.
And for this—
The nation rendered to him a flower
A little thing—a flower
Aye, but yet not so little
For this flower grew in the nation's heart
A wet, soft blossom
From tears of her who loved her son
Even when the black battle rages
Made his face the face of furious urchin,
And this she cherished
And finally laid it upon the breast of him.
A little thing—this flower?
No—it was the flower of duty
That inhales black smoke-clouds
And fastens it's roots in bloody sod
And yet comes forth so fair, so fragrant—
It's birth is sunlight in grimest, darkest place.

*125*      A row of thick pillars
Consciously bracing for the weight
Of a vanished roof
The bronze light of sunset strikes through them,
And over a floor made for slow rites.
There is no sound of singing
But, aloft, a great and terrible bird
Is watching a cur, beaten and cut,
That crawls to the cool shadows of the pillars
To die.

126    Oh, a rare old wine ye brewed for me
       Flagons of despair
       A deep deep drink of this wine of life
       Flagons of despair.

            Dream of riot and blood and screams
            The rolling white eyes of dying men
            The terrible heedless courage of babes

127     There exists the eternal fact of conflict
And—next—a mere sense of locality.
Afterward we derive sustenance from the winds.
Afterward we grip upon this sense of locality.
Afterward, we become patriots.
The godly vice of patriotism makes us slaves,
And—let us surrender to this falsity
Let us be patriots

Then welcome us the practical men
Thrumming on a thousand drums
The practical men, God help us.
    They cry aloud to be led to war
    Ah—
    They have been poltroons on a thousand fields
    And the sacked sad city of New York is their record
    Furious to face the Spaniard, these people, and
        crawling worms before their task
    They name serfs and send charity in bulk to better
        men
    They play at being free, these people of New York
    Who are too well-dressed to protest against infamy

128     On the brown trail
        We hear the grind of your carts
        To our villages,
        Laden with food
        Laden with food
        We know you are come to our help
        But—
        Why do you impress upon us
        Your foriegn happiness?
        We know it not.
        (Hark!
        Carts laden with food
        Laden with food)
        We weep because we dont understand
        But your gifts form into a yoke
        The food turns into a yoke
        (Hark!
        Carts laden with food
        Laden with food)
        It is our mission to vanish
        Grateful because of full mouths
        Destiny—Darkness
        Time understands
        And ye—ye bigoted men of a moment—
        —Wait—
        Await your turn.

129     All-feeling God, hear in the war-night
The rolling voices of a nation;
Through dusky billows of darkness
See the flash, the under-light, of bared swords—
—Whirling gleams like wee shells
Deep in the streams of the universe—
Bend and see a people, O, God,
A people rebuked, accursed,
By him of the many lungs
And by him of the bruised weary war-drum
    (The chanting disintegrate and the two-faced eagle)
Bend and mark our steps, O, God.
Mark well, mark well, Father of the Never-Ending Circles
And if the path, the new path, lead awry
Then in the forest of the lost standards
Suffer us to grope and bleed apace
For the wisdom is thine.
Bend and see a people, O, God,
A people applauded, acclaimed,
By him of the raw red shoulders
The manacle-marked, the thin victim
(He lies white amid the smoking cane)

[NO STANZA BREAK]

—And if the path, the new path, leads straight—
Then—O, God—then bare the great bronze arm;
Swing high the blaze of the chained stars
And let them look and heed
 (The chanting disintegrate and the two-faced eagle)
For we go, we go in a lunge of a long blue corps
And—to Thee we commit our lifeless sons,
The convulsed and furious dead.
 (They shall be white amid the smoking cane)
For, the seas shall not bar us;
The capped mountains shall not hold us back
We shall sweep and swarm through jungle and pool,
Then let the savage one bend his high chin
To see on his breast, the sullen glow of the death-medals
For we know and we say our gift.
His prize is death, deep doom.
 (He shall be white amid the smoking cane)

130    A grey and boiling street
Alive with rickety noise.
Suddenly, a hearse,
Trailed by black carriages
Takes a deliberate way
Through this chasm of commerce;
And children look eagerly
To find the misery behind the shades.
Hired men, impatient, drive with a longing
To reach quickly the grave-side, the end of
    solemnity.

Yes, let us have it over.
Drive, man, drive.
Flog your sleek-hided beasts,
Gallop—gallop—gallop.
Let us finish it quickly.

131 Bottles and bottles and bottles
In a merry den
And the wan smiles of women
Untruthing license and joy.
Countless lights
Making oblique and confusing multiplication
In mirrors
And the light returns again to the faces.

\*   \*   \*   \*   \*   \*   \*   \*   \*   \*   \*

A cellar, and a death-pale child.
A woman
Ministering commonly, degradedly,
Without manners.
A murmur and a silence
Or silence and a murmur
And then a finished silence.
The moon beams practically upon the cheap bed.

An hour, with it's million trinkets of joy or
  pain,
Matters little in cellar or merry den
Since all is death.

*132*    intermingled,
There come in wild revelling strains
Black words, stinging
That murder flowers
The horror of profane speculation.

133    The patent of a lord
       And the bangle of a bandit
       Make argument
       Which God solves
       Only after lighting more candles.

*134*  Tell me not in joyous numbers
We can make our lives sublime
By—well, at least, not by
Dabbling much in rhyme.

*135*      My cross!

        Your cross?
        The real cross
        Is made of pounds,
        Dollars or francs.
        Here I bear my palms for the silly nails
        To teach the lack
        —The great pain of lack—
        Of coin.

*THE BIBLIOGRAPHIES*

Locations of items in these sections are abbreviated as follows:

NNC  Special Collections, Butler Library, Columbia University

InU  Lilly Library, Indiana University

NcU  University of North Carolina Library

NSyU  Lena R. Arents Rare Book Room, Syracuse University Library

ViU  Alderman Library, University of Virginia

A. PUBLICATIONS

Items in this section are periodical appearances and separate publications of the poems, arranged chronologically and numbered. Each entry contains (1) the conventional enumerative bibliographical description, (2) pertinent identifying remarks, (3) reference to standard bibliographies when possible,* and (4) an identification of the poems in the item through reference to the List of Poems.

---

* The standard bibliography is Ames W. Williams and Vincent Starrett, *Stephen Crane: A Bibliography* (Glendale, California, 1948), as supplemented by Jacob Blanck, *Bibliography of American Literature*, Vol. II (New Haven, 1957), pp. 329-338, and Joseph Katz, "Toward a Descriptive Bibliography of Stephen Crane: *The Black Riders,*" *Papers of the Bibliographical Society of America*, LIX (Second Quarter 1965), 150-157.

1. *The Black Riders and Other Lines by Stephen Crane.* Boston: Copeland and Day, 1895. The first impression of the first edition. Williams and Starrett 2a; Blanck 4070. *1-68.*

2. *The Black Riders and Other Lines by Stephen Crane.* Boston: Copeland and Day, 1895. A printing in green ink on "Japan" paper advertised as limited to fifty trade copies and reported as existing in three copies bound in vellum; printed at the same time and from the same standing of type as Publication 1. Williams and Starrett 2b; Blanck 4070 (as Japan Paper Editions A and B) . *1-68.*

3. *Philistine*, I, 3 (August, 1895), [93]. *94.*

4. *Philistine*, I, 4 (September, 1895), 124. *101.*

5. *"The Time Has Come," The Walrus Said, "To Talk of Many Things."* East Aurora, New York: The Roycroft Printing Shop, 1895, p. [8]. Souvenir menu of the Philistine's dinner in honor of Crane. Williams and Starrett 5; Blanck 4072. *82.*

6. *Philistine*, II, 1 (December, 1895), [9]. *89.*

7. *The Black Riders and Other Lines by Stephen Crane.* Boston and London: Copeland and Day and William Heinemann, 1896. Although marked "Third Edition," this is actually the second impression of the first edition. Williams and Starrett 2c. *1-68.*

8. *Philistine*, II, 2 (January, 1896), 62. *82.*

9. *Bookman*, II, 6 (February, 1896) , 476. *76.*

10. *Philistine*, II, 3 (February, 1896), [94-95]. *77.*

11. *Chap-Book*, IV, 8 (March, 1896), 372. *93.*

12. *Philistine*, II, 5 (April, 1896), [152]. *78.*

13. "A Souvenir and a Medley: Seven Poems and a Sketch by Stephen Crane." *The Roycroft Quarterly*, I (May, 1896),

[2], 27-37. There are actually eight poems by Crane. Williams and Starrett 5; Blanck 4074. *24, 94, 101, 89, 82, 77, 78, 83.*

14. *Bookman,* III, 3 (May, 1896), 196-97, 206. *9, 10, 69-73.*

15. *Philistine,* III, 1 (June, 1896), [20]. *83.*

16. *Bookman,* IV, 2 (October, 1896) , 149. *81.*

17. *The Black Riders and Other Lines by Stephen Crane.* London: William Heinemann, 1896. The first English edition. Williams and Starrett 11. *1-68.*

18. *Philistine,* VI, 3 (February, 1898), [back wrapper]. *95.*

19. *Philistine,* VI, 5 (April, 1898), [back wrapper]. *85.*

20. *Philistine,* VI, 6 (May, 1898) , 166-67. *86.*

21. *Philistine,* VII, 1 (June, 1898), 9-10. *74.*

22. *Philistine,* VIII, 1 (December, 1898), [front wrapper]. *75.*

23. *Spanish-American War Songs: A Complete Collection of Newspaper Verse Published During the Recent War With Spain.* Sidney A. Witherbee, ed. Detroit, Michigan: Sidney A. Witherbee, 1898. Williams and Starrett 28; Blanck 4082. *74.*

24. *War Is Kind by Stephen Crane.* New York: Frederick A. Stokes Company, 1899. The first edition. Williams and Starrett 20; Blanck 4083. *76-102.*

25. *Philistine,* VIII, 4 (March, 1899) , [back wrapper]. *9.*

26. *Philistine,* IX, 5 (October, 1899), 149-50. *95.*

27. *An American Anthology: 1787-1899. Selections Illustrating the Editor's Critical Review of American Poetry in the Nineteenth Century.* Edmund Clarence Stedman, ed. Boston and New York: Houghton, Mifflin and Company, 1900, pp. 733-34. *93, 65, 1, 25, 88, 27, 22, 98, 81.*

28. *Wounds in the Rain: War Stories by Stephen Crane*. New York: Frederick A. Stokes Company, 1900, p. 42. The first American edition. Williams and Starrett 28; Blanck 4091. *117.*

29. *The Black Riders and Other Lines by Stephen Crane*. [Boston]: "Privately reprinted by courtesy of Small, Maynard and Company," 1905. *1-68.*

30. *The Black Riders and Other Lines*. In *The Work of Stephen Crane*, Vol. VI. Wilson Follett, ed., Amy Lowell, intro. New York: Alfred A. Knopf, 1926. Reprinted New York: Russell and Russell, 1963. Williams and Starrett 38; Blanck 4101. *1-68, 76-98, 100-102, 74, 103-112.*

31. *Bookman*, LXIX, 2 (April, 1929), 120-122. *113-115.*

32. *The Collected Poems of Stephen Crane*. Wilson Follett, ed. New York and London: Alfred A. Knopf, 1930. Williams and Starrett 39; Blanck 4103. *1-68, 76-98, 100-102, 74, 103-115.*

33. *A Lost Poem by Stephen Crane*. New York: The Harvard Press, [1933]. "Of this first printing one hundred copies have been issued for the friends of Harvey Taylor." Reprinted in *The Golden Book*, XIX (February, 1934), 189. Williams and Starrett 45; Blanck 4105. *116.*

34. *The Poetry of Stephen Crane*. By Daniel G. Hoffman. New York: Columbia University Press, 1957, pp. 41, 75-76, 78, 84-85, 88-89, 118, 132-33, 138-39, 149, 156-59, 183-85, 283-84. *118-135.*

B. DRAFT MATERIAL

Manuscripts, typescripts, and corrected copies are arranged in the order of the poetry in the List of Poems, and are assigned letters of the alphabet. Although occasional drafts contain more than one poem, the poem has been considered the unit of identification. Conjugate drafts are as follows: L, M; Y, B$^1$; C$^1$, D$^1$. Drafts which evidently were conjugate at the time of preparation but which subsequently have been disjuncted are as follows: T, V, X; O, P, R; P$^1$, Q$^1$. Each entry contains the (1) first line as it appears in the draft, (2) the type of item (manuscript, fair copy, corrected page of a publication, corrected proof, or typescript), (3) additional identifying remarks when pertinent, (4) the location of the item, and (5) an identification of the poem. An asterisk (*) at the end of an entry indicates that the item is a copy prepared by Cora Crane.

A.   Three little birds in a row
     Ms. inscribed at head: "[Within a circle] 2 1/4 in. | I."
     (Baum, *Exhibition,* item 38). ViU. *2.*

B.   I looked here | I looked there
     Ms. inscribed: "509 cat 28 Jl 54 | # VIII In Black Riders,
     last lines 'She is none so fair as she | In my heart' (as |
     printed) ." NSyU. *8.*

C.   Should the wide world roll away
     Ms. inscribed: "[At head] 11 | [At foot] no. X | 507 Orig-
     inal 'Black Riders' lines—ms. Stephen Crane 1894."
     NSyU. *10.*

D.   In Heaven,
     Ms. inscribed: "[At head] #XVIII | 61 | [At foot] 508 cat
     28 Jl 54." NSyU. *18.*

E.   There was One I met upon the road
     Ms. NNC. *33.*

F.  When a people reach the top of a hill
Ms. NNC. *74.*

G.  Hoarse booming drums of the regiment
Fair copy (?) laid in a copy of *The Red Badge of Courage;*
inscribed at foot: "Stephen Crane | Washington, D. C. |
March 18, 1896." ViU. *76.*

H.  "Do not weep, maiden, for war is kind
Fair copy on the recto of the third leaf of *The Red Badge
of Courage* presented to William Dean Howells and mis-
dated "—1895—." (Baum, *Exhibition,* item 49). NN. *76.*

I.  Do not weep, maiden, for war is kind.
Ts. entitled "WAR IS KIND." NNC. *76.*

J.  "What says the sea, little shell?
Ms. (3 ff.) entitled (title obliterated) and inscribed: "[At
head of f.1] The Shell and the Pines. | [At foot of f.3]
Stephen Crane." The pages are numbered, and p. 2 has
been marked by printer for small capitals for stanza 4.
NN. *77.*

K.  "What says the sea, little shell?
Fair copy (2 ff.) tipped into a copy of *The Red Badge of
Courage;* presented to Dr. A. L. Mitchell inscribed: "[At
foot of f. 2] Stephen Crane | To my friend, Dr. A. L.
Mitchell. | Hartwood, N. Y. Dec. 28, 1895." InU. *77.*

L.  "What says the sea, little shell?
Ts. conjugate with, and preceding, Draft M, marked: "[At
foot] (The Philistine) ." NNC. *77.*

M.  To the maiden
Ts. conjugate with, and succeeding, Draft L, marked: "[At
foot] (The Philistine)." NNC. *78.*

N.  What?
Ms. inscribed: "[At foot] Stephen Crane | Oh, Hubbard
[Elbert Hubbard of *The Philistine*], mark this well. Mark
it well! If | it is over-balancing your discretion, inform me.

| S. C." This manuscript was reproduced in *The Fra*, July 1910, p. xxv. NSyU. *79*.

O.  A little ink more or less!
    Ts. "[At foot] (The Philistine)." NNC. *79*.

P.  "Have you ever made a just man?"
    Ts., evidently at one time the upper portion of a leaf of which Draft R was the lower portion. NNC. *80*.

Q.  I Explain the silvered path of a ship at night
    Ms. NNC. *81*.

R.  I explain the silvered passing of a ship at night,
    Ts., evidently at one time the lower portion of a leaf of which Draft P was the upper portion. NNC. *81*.

S.  I explain the silvered path of a ship at night
    Ts., marked "-2-" at the head, and inscribed in Cora Crane's hand: "[In upper left corner] War is Kind." NNC. *81*.*

T.  I have heard the sunset song of the birches
    Ts. marked: "[At foot] (The Philistine)." NNC. *82*.

U.  Fast rode the knight—
    Ms., signed: "Stephen Crane." NSyU. *83*.

V.  Fast rode the knight
    Ts. marked: [At foot] (The Philistine)." NNC. *83*.

W.  Forth went the candid man
    Ms. NNC. *84*.

X.  Forth went the candid man
    Ts. NNC. *84*.

Y.  You tell me this is God?
    Ts. conjugate with and preceding, Draft B¹, marked: "[At foot] (The Philistine)." NNC. *85*.

Z.  On the desert
    Ms. inscribed: "[At foot] Stephen Crane | (See May 1898 | Philistine) | (The Philistine) | Please send proof." ViU. *86*.

$A^1$.    On the desert
Corrected proof sheet for Publication 20 inscribed in an unidentified hand: "[In lower left corner] Proof for | correction for | May Philistine." NNC. *86*.

$B^1$.    On the desert
Ts. conjugate with, and succeeding, Draft Y. NNC. *86*.

$C^1$.    The wayfarer
Ts. conjugate with, and preceding, Draft $D^1$. NNC. *88*.

$D^1$.    A slant of sun on dull brown walls
Ts. conjugate with, and succeeding, Draft $C^1$, marked: "[At foot] (The Philistine)." NNC. *89*.

$E^1$.    Once, a man, clambering to the house-tops,
Ms. on verso of f.6 of ms. of "Gratitude, the sense of obligation" (see Appendix I), inscribed: "Stephen Crane | Hartwood Club | Port Jervis N. Y. | [Inverted at the foot] The name of this club | shall be the." NNC. *90*.

$F^1$.    Once a man clambering to the housetops
Ms. NNC. *90*.

$G^1$.    There was a man with tongue of wood
Ms. NNC. *91*.

$H^1$.    The successful man has thrust himself through the water of the years
Ms. inscribed: "[At foot] Stephen Crane | Dec 5th, 1897." NNC. *92*.

$I^1$.    The successful man has thrust himself
Ts. NNC. *92*.

$J^1$.    In the night
Ms. inscribed: "[In upper left corner] Stephen Crane | Hartwood | Sullivan Co. | N. Y. | [At foot] Stephen Crane." Tipped into *The Chap-Book*, IV, 8 (March, 1896), enclosed in a leather binder labelled *Verses and Original Manuscript*. NcU. *93*.

K¹.   In the night
Corrected page of Publication 11 (see Baum, *Exhibition,* item 103). NNC. *93.*

L¹.   In the night
Ts. marked: "[At foot] (The Chap-book)." NNC. *93.*

M¹.   The chatter of a death-demon from a tree-top.
Ts. marked: "[At foot] (The Philistine)." NNC. *94.*

N¹.   The impact of a dollar upon the heart
Ts. inscribed in Cora Crane's hand: "[At head] By | Stephen Crane." NNC. *95.*

O¹.   When the prophet, a complacent fat man,
Ts. NNC. *97.*

P¹.   Aye, workman, make me a dream
Ts. NNC. *100.*

Q¹.   Each small gleam was a voice
Ts. "[At foot] (The Philistine)." NNC. *101.*

R¹.   The trees in the garden rained flowers.
Ts. NNC. *102.*

S¹.   Thou art my love | And thou art the peace of sundown
Ts. entitled: "[At head] Intrigue." NNC. *103.*

T¹.   Thou art my love | And thou art a storm
Ts. NNC. *103.*

U¹.   Thou art my love | And thou art a tinsel thing
Ts. NNC. *103.*

V¹.   Thou art my love | And thou are a weary violet.
Ts. NNC. *103.*

W¹.   Thou art my love | And thou art the ashes of other men's
Ts. NNC. *103.*

X¹.   Thou art my love | And thou art the beard
Ts. NNC. *103.*

Y$^1$.    Thou art my love | And thou art a temple
Ts. NNC. *103*.

Z$^1$.    Thou art my love | And thou art a wretch.
Ts. NNC. *103*.

A$^2$.    Thou art my love | And thou art a priestess
Ts. NNC. *103*.

B$^2$.    Thou art my love | And thou art a skull with ruby eyes
Ts. NNC. *103*.

C$^2$.    Thou art my love | And I doubt thee
Ts. NNC. *103*.

D$^2$.    Thou art my love | And thou art death
Ts. NNC. *103*.

E$^2$.    Love forgive me if I wish you grief
Ts. marked: "[In lower right corner] 1." NNC. *104*.

F$^2$.    You walk among men
Ts. marked: "[In lower right corner] 11." NNC. *104*.

G$^2$.    He had your picture in his room
Ts. marked: "[In lower right corner] 111." NNC. *104*.

H$^2$.    Fool, not to know that thy little shoe
Ts. marked: "[In lower right corner] 1V." NNC. *104*.

I$^2$.    God give me medals
Ts. NNC. *104*.

J$^2$.    Now let me crunch you
Ts. NNC. *104*.

K$^2$.    Beware of my friends
Ts. marked: "[In lower right corner] V11." NNC. *104*.

L$^2$.    The flower I gave thee once
Ts. marked: "[In lower right corner] V111." NNC. *104*.

M$^2$.    Ah, God, the way your little finger moved
Ts. marked: "[In lower right corner] 1X." NNC. *105*.

N². Once I saw thee idly rocking
Ts. NNC. *106.*

O². Tell me why, behind thee,
Ts. marked: "[In lower right corner] X1." NNC. *107.*

P². A man adrift on a slim spar
Ms. signed: "[At foot] Stephen Crane." (reproduced in Publication 31) . NNC. *113.*

Q². A man adrift on a slim spar
Holograph copy in Cora's hand, inscribed: "[At head] *4.* | [At foot] (Copy) Stephen Crane." NNC. *113.**

R². Chant you loud of punishments
Ms. NNC. *114.*

S². Chant you loud of punishments
Ts. marked "-1-" at head and inscribed in Cora Crane's hand: "[In upper left corner] Not used in US." NNC. *114.**

T². A naked woman and a dead dwarf;
Ts. NNC. *115.*

U². Little birds of the night
Ms. (2 pp.) in *Stephen Crane's Notebook.* ViU. *116.*

V². In a large vaulted hall that blazed with light
Ms. NSyU. *118.*

W². One came from the skies
Ms. NNC. *119.*

X². One came from the skies
Ts. marked "-8-" at head. NNC. *119.**

Y². A god came to a man
Ms. (2 ff.). NNC. *120.*

Z². A god came to a man
Ts. (2 ff.) marked "-6-" at head of f. 1, and "-7-" at head of f. 2; both markings obliterated and notations in Cora Crane's hand substituted: "[At head of f. 1] (1) | [At head of f. 2] (2)." NNC. *120.**

A³.  There is a grey thing that lives in the tree-tops
     Ms. NNC. *121.*

B³.  There is a grey thing that lives in the tree-tops
     Ts. marked "-5-" at head. NNC. *121.**

C³.  If you would seek a friend among men
     Ms. NNC. *122.*

D³.  If you would seek a friend among men
     Ts. marked "-3-" at head; inscribed in Cora Crane's hand:
     "[In upper left corner] Not used in war is kind." NNC. *122.**

E³.  A lad and a maid at a curve in the stream
     Ms. NNC. *123.*

F³.  A lad and a maid at a curve in the stream
     Ts. marked "-4-" at head. NNC. *123.**

G³.  A soldier, young in years, young in ambitions
     Ms., f. 1 of "Gratitude, the sense of obligation" (see
     Appendix I) . NNC. *124.*

H³.  A row of thick pillars
     Ts. NNC. *125.*

I³.  Oh, a rare old wine ye brewed for me
     Ms. NNC. *126.*

J³.  Oh, a rare old wine ye brewed for me
     Ms. in Cora Crane's hand, inscribed: "[At head] *3* - [At
     foot] Stephen Crane | Copy." NNC. *126.**

K³.  There exists the eternal fact of conflict
     Ms. NNC. *127.*

L³.  On the brown trail
     Ms. NNC. *128.*

M³.  On the brown trail
     Holograph copy by Cora Crane, inscribed: "[At head] *2* |
     [At foot] Stephen Crane | (Copy)." NNC. *128.**

N³.  All-feeling God, hear in the war-night
Ts. and carbon copy (2 ff. each) marked: "[At head of f. 1]
THE BATTLE HYMN | BY. | STEPHEN CRANE |
[At foot of f. 2] (The ms., of the above, has just been dis-
covered in saddle-bags used by Stephen Crane during the
late war with Spain.)." NNC. *129.*\*

O³.  A grey and boiling street
Ts. NNC. *130.*

P³.  Bottles and bottles and bottles
Ts. NNC. *131.*

Q³.  intermingled,
Ms. NNC. *132.*

R³.  The patent of a lord
Ms. NNC. *133.*

S³.  Tell me not in joyous numbers
Ms. on the verso of a sheet inscribed: "To the editor of the
Gazette, Sir: - | I compelled to | enter a feeble and totter-
ing protest." NNC. *134.*

T³.  MY CROSS!
Ts. NNC. *135.*

U³.  My cross!
Ts. NNC. *135.*

*NOTES*

## THE BLACK RIDERS AND OTHER LINES

The dedication, "TO HAMLIN GARLAND," appeared in Publication 1, 2, 7, and 17, and is incorporated in a preliminary statement to the first section of Publication 30 (p. [xxxi]): "THIS GROUP IS SUBSTANTIALLY | A REPRINT OF | THE BLACK RIDERS AND OTHER LINES | PUBLISHED 1895 | AND | DEDICATED TO HAMLIN GARLAND." Apparently, Crane's gesture was an afterthought suggested by a re-reading of Garland's laudatory review of *Maggie*. "I had no dedication in mind for the volume but on second thoughts I would like to dedicate it to Hamlin Garland in just one line, no more: TO HAMLIN GARLAND." (Three months after the book appeared, Crane asked Garland, "Do you care?" See Stallman and Gilkes, *Letters*, pp. 47, 59-60.)

The assumption that Crane wrote the poems for the volume in one intensive burst of creation appears to be acceptable. Pizer's "The Garland-Crane Relationship," a reconciliation of Garland's accounts of his meetings with Crane, agrees with Fryckstedt's conclusion in "Crane's *Black Riders*: A Discussion of Dates" that the poems were probably written in the Winter of 1893-1894.

Note that four editions of *The Black Riders* mentioned in the literature appear to be ghosts. Starrett, *Stephen Crane: A Bibliography*, p. 14, lists a "N. Y. edition . . . marked 'Third Edition;'" this is evidently an erroneous listing of Publication

7. Perhaps it is this that Stolper, *Stephen Crane: A List of His Writings,* p. 16, notes as "N. Y. Privately printed, 1912. Reprint by a group in Washington Square." In addition, Stolper includes in his *List* an edition published in London by Heinemann in 1895. Williams and Starrett, *Stephen Crane: A Bibliography,* p. 86, notes the last of the editions that cannot be found, a volume published in Boston by Sherman, French & Company in 1912.

## *1*

Late in September, 1894, Crane suggested that the volume be titled after the poem "beginning 'Black riders rode forth,' etc." (See Baum, *Stephen Crane: An Exhibition,* p. 20.) But on 30 October, Crane sent Copeland and Day a "copy of title poem." (See Stallman and Gilkes, *Letters,* p. 40.) The implication is either that Copeland and Day had lost the original manuscript, or that Crane had revised the poem within the month.

| | |
|---|---|
| *Versions* | 1, 2, 7, 17, 27, 29, 30, 32. |
| *Text* | [*Title*] THE BLACK RIDERS ] 27. |
| 1. | . . .Riders ] 29. |
| 6. | . . . sin. ] 27. |

While Beer, *Stephen Crane,* pp. 38-39, suggests that the poem derives from a childhood dream of "black riders on black horses charging at him from the long surf up the shore," the Four Horsemen of the Apocalypse in Revelations 6: 2, 4, 5, 8 appear to have more relevance. (The rider of the black horse carried a pair of balances.) "Sin" (line 6) here apparently is personified.

## *2*

| | |
|---|---|
| *Versions* | A, 1, 2, 7, 17, 29, 30, 32. |

*Text*
3.   . . . place ] A.
4-5.   [*No break*] ] 29.
5.   . . . SAID, "HE ] 1, 2, 7, 17. . . . said, "He ]
     29, 30, 32.
6.   . . . laugh, ] 29.
9.   . . . curious ] A.

*3*

*Versions*   1, 2, 7, 17, 29, 30, 32.
*Text*
6.   . . . SAID, "IS ] 1, 2, 7, 17. . . . said, "Is ] 29,
     30, 32.

*4*

*Versions*   1, 2, 7, 17, 29, 30, 32.

*5*

*Versions*   1, 2, 7, 17, 29, 30, 32.
*Text*
2.   . . . SAID, ] 1, 2, 7, 17. . . . said, ] 29, 30, 32.

5.   . . . CLAMOUR ] 7, 17.   . . . clamour ] 30,
     32.
13.   . . . STAID ] 1, 2, 7, 17. . . . staid ] 29.

"Staid" (line 13) has been considered an error in orthography although it is given as an alternate spelling for "stayed" in *An American Dictionary of the English Language* (Springfield, 1855) , p. 1074. Crane characteristically used the conventional spelling of the past tense of "to stay." See also *32*, line 8.

6

| Versions | 1, 2, 7, 17, 29, 30, 32. |
|---|---|
| Text | |
| 1. | . . . carefully ] 29. |
| 2. | . . . All-Master ] 29, 30, 32. |
| 6. | . . . his ] 29. |
| 7. | . . . Wrong ] 29. |
| 11. | . . . for ever ] 30, 32. |

7

| Versions | 1, 2, 7, 17, 29, 30, 32. |
|---|---|
| Text | |
| 1. | . . . Shadow, ] 29. |
| 7. | . . . quaver. ] 30, 32. |

8

| Versions | B, 1, 2, 7, 17, 29, 30, 32. |
|---|---|
| Text | |
| 1. | . . . here ] B. |
| 2. | And [*cancelled*] I . . . there ] B. |
| 3. | No where ] B. |
| 6. | Truly then I . . . complaint ] B. |
| 7. | . . . 'though . . . fairer ] B. |
| 8. | She is none so fair ] B. |
| 9. | As herself in my heart. ] B. |

9

| Versions | 1, 2, 7, 14, 17, 25, 29, 30, 32. |
|---|---|
| Text | |
| 1. | . . . High Place, ] 25. |
| 2. | . . . Devils ] 25. |

4.     . . . Sin. ] 25.
6.     . . . SAID, "COMRADE! ] 1, 2, 7, 14, 17. . . .
       said, "Comrade! ] 25, 29, 30, 32.

Publication 14 reprints this poem, and poem *10,* from the first edition as part of a blurb on the illustrator of "Legends" (*69-73*) , Mélanie Elisabeth Norton:

> We feel a proper editorial pride in giving our readers in this number a chance to see a specimen of the work of Miss Mélanie Elisabeth Norton, a young artist of this city [New York], who has made the marginal illustrations to Mr. Stephen Crane's "Legends" on page 206. Miss Norton has caught to perfection the spirit of Mr. Crane's unique imaginings, and the truth of this is even better seen in the reproduction given above of her designs for two of his poems from *The Black Riders.* As grotesque as anything of Aubrey Beardsley, they have a thought and a meaning that his work often lacks, and are fairly startling in their weirdly imaginative power. We predict for Miss Norton an immediate vogue and a brilliant future.

Publication 25 is a similar coupling: *9* is printed with a Denslow cartoon of Crane in tails being peered at by a sophisticated Devil. This is reproduced in Felix Shay, *Elbert Hubbard of East Aurora,* p. 379. (See also Denslow's "Lines to Pegasus and Stephen Crane" in Shay, p. 364.)

*10*

*Versions*     C, 1, 2, 7, 14, 17, 29, 30, 32.
  *Text*
    1.     . . . away ] C.
    2.     . . . terror ] C.
    5.     . . . essential ] C.
    6.     . . . there ] C.

For Publication 14, see the note to *9*.

Beer, *Stephen Crane*, pp. 64-65, is the source of a note from Crane to Helen Trent (Stallman and Gilkes, *Letters*, p. 10, dates the note as 20 September 1891) which is an analogue to this poem:

> You have the most beautiful arms I ever saw. You never should have to wear dresses with sleeves. If I could keep your arms nothing else would count. It would not matter if there was nothing else to hope for in the world or if there was no more world. In dreams, don't you ever fall and fall but not be afraid of anything because somebody safe is with you? I shall be here to-morrow. I must get back to Ed's house [Edmund Crane, Stephen's brother, lived in Lake View, New Jersey], now.

*11*

| Versions | 1, 2, 7, 17, 29, 30, 32. |
|---|---|
| Text | |
| 8. | Ay, ] 30, 32. |
| 9. | . . . ONCE, ] 1, 2, 7, 17. . . . once, ] 29, 30, 32. |

*12*

| Versions | 1, 2, 7, 17, 29, 30, 32. |
|---|---|
| Text | |
| Ep. | "and ] 29. |
| 1. | . . . thee, Unrighteous Picture; ] 29. |
| 2. | . . . Image, . . . thee; ] 29. |
| 3. | . . . thy ] 29. |

The epigraph is drawn from Exodus 20: 5:

> Thou shalt not bow down thyself to them [graven images], nor serve them: for I the LORD thy God *am*

> a jealous God, visiting the iniquity of the fathers upon the children unto the third and fourth *generation* of them that hate me;

### 13

| | |
|---|---|
| *Versions* | 1, 2, 7, 17, 29, 30, 32. |

### 14

| | |
|---|---|
| *Versions* | 1, 2, 7, 17, 29, 30, 32. |
| *Text* | |
| 6. | ...SAID, "WHY ] 1, 2, 7, 17. ... said, "Why ] 29, 30, 32. |
| 8. | ...CLAMOUR ]7, 17. ... clamour ] 30, 32. |

### 15

| | |
|---|---|
| *Versions* | 1, 2, 7, 17, 29, 30, 32. |
| *Text* | |
| 2. | ... TALES,— ] 1, 2, 7, 17. ... tales,— ] 30, 32. |

### 16

| | |
|---|---|
| *Versions* | 1, 2, 7, 17, 29, 30, 32. |

### 17

| | |
|---|---|
| *Versions* | 1, 2, 7, 17, 29, 30, 32. |

### 18

| | |
|---|---|
| *Versions* | D, 1, 2, 7, 17, 29, 30, 32. |
| *Text* | |
| 1. | ... heaven, ] 30, 32. |
| 4. | "And [*cancelled*] "What ] D. |
| 4-5. | All the little blades [*cancelled*] ] D. |

5.      All save one | Of the little blades ] D.
8.      . . . little [*cancelled*] small [*substituted*] way ] D.
10.     Presently God ] D. . . . SAID, ] 1, 2, 7, 17. . . . said, ] 29, 30, 32.
11.     "And [*inserted subsequently*] what . . . *you* [*italics deleted*] do?" ] D.
12.     . . . ANSWERED, "OH, ] 1, 2, 7, 17. . . . answered, "Oh, ] 29. . . . answered, "O my lord, ] 30, 32. . . . "My lord, ] D.
14.     For if . . . deeds ] D.
16.     . . . God in . . . splendor ] D. . . . splendour, ] 30, 32.
18.     "O best ] 30, 32. . . . grass," He ] D.

## 19

*Versions*  1, 2, 7, 17, 29, 30, 32.
*Text*
9.      . . . CRIED, ] 1, 2, 7, 17. . . . cried, ] 29, 30, 32.

## 20

*Versions*  1, 2, 7, 17, 29, 30, 32.
*Text*
2.      . . . SAID, "I ] 1, 2, 7, 17. . . . said, "I ] 29, 30, 32, way—come" ] 30, 32.
9.      . . . CRIED, "I ] 1, 2, 7, 17. . . . cried, "I ] 29, 30, 32.

## 21

*Versions*  1, 2, 7, 17, 29, 30, 32.

22

| | |
|---|---|
| *Versions* | 1, 2, 7, 17, 29, 30, 32. |
| *Text* | [*Title*] ANCESTRY ] 27. |
| 1. | . . . Mountains ] 29. |
| 4. | Ay, ] 27, 30, 32. |
| 5. | . . . ME, ] 1, 2, 7, 17. . . . me, ] 27, 29, 30, 32. |
| 9. | . . . grandfathers— ] 30, 32. |
| 11. | . . . Mountains. ] 29. |

23

| | |
|---|---|
| *Versions* | 1, 2, 7, 17, 29, 30, 32. |

24

| | |
|---|---|
| *Versions* | 1, 2, 7, 13, 17, 29, 30, 32. |
| *Text* | |
| 5. | . . . futile" I ] 13. |
| 6. | . . . NEVER"— ] 1, 2, 7, 17. . . . never"— ] 29. |

In Publication 13, the poem is followed by an ascription, "—*The Black Riders.*" Since this appearance is on a preliminary page, since the ascription was appended to the poem, and since this poem is not recorded in the subtitle to the volume ("Seven Poems and a Sketch by Stephen Crane"), it is probable that *24* was adapted by Elbert Hubbard from *The Black Riders* and therefore carries no authority.

25

| | |
|---|---|
| *Versions* | 1, 2, 7, 17, 27, 29, 30, 32. |
| *Text* | [*Title*] WHY? ] 27. |

**26**

Versions      1, 2, 7, 17, 29, 30, 32.
    Text
      5.      . . . LABOUR ] 7, 17. . . . labour ] 30, 32.

**27**

Versions      1, 2, 7, 17, 27, 29, 30, 32.
   Text      [*Title*] CONTENT ] 27.

**28**

Versions      1, 2, 7, 17, 29, 30, 32.

**29**

Versions      1, 2, 7, 17, 29, 30, 32.
    Text
      8.      . . . HIM, ] 1, 2, 7, 17. . . . him, ] 29.
             . . . Him, ] 30, 32.
     10.     . . . SLOWLY, ] 1, 2, 7, 17. . . . slowly, ] 29, 30, 32.

**30**

Versions      1, 2, 7, 17, 29, 30, 32.

**31**

Versions      1, 2, 7, 17, 29, 30, 32.

**32**

Versions      1, 2, 7, 17, 29, 30, 32.

**33**

Versions      E, 1, 2, 7, 17, 24, 29, 30, 32.

*Text*

1.      . . . one ] 24, 29, 30, 32.

3.      . . . SAID, "SHOW ] 1, 2, 7, 17. . . . said, "Show ] 29, 30, 32.

4.      And this I ] E, 29, 30, 32. AND THIS I ] 1, 2, 7, 17.

6.      . . . SAID, "IT ] 1, 2, 7, 17. . . . said, "It ] 29, 30, 32.

7.      . . . held I ] E, 29, 30, 32. . . . HELD I . . . ANOTHER, ] 1, 2, 7, 17. . . . another; ] 29, 30, 32.

8.      . . . SAID, "IT ] 1, 2, 7, 17. . . . said, "It ] 29, 30, 32.

9.      . . . held I ] E, 29, 30, 32. . . . HELD I . . . ANOTHER; ] 1, 2, 7, 17. . . . another ] E. . . . another; ] 29, 30, 32.

10.     . . . SAID, "IT ] 1, 2, 7, 17. . . . said, "It ] 29, 30, 32.

11.     . . . end ] E. . . . END; ] 1, 2, 7, 17. . . . end; ] 29, 30, 32.

12.     . . . he . . . sin!" ] E. . . . SAID, IT ] 1, 2, 7, 17. . . . he said, "It ] 29, 30, 32.

13.     At the end I ] E. AND, FINALLY, I . . . OUT, ] 1, 2, 7, 17. And, finally, I . . . out, ] 29, 30, 32.

15.     Then did He [*capitalized subsequently*] look at ] E.

17.     . . . SOUL!" HE ] 1, 2, 7, 17. . . . soul!" He ] E. . . . he ] 24, 29, 30, 32.

No draft of this poem survives in the typescript that Crane prepared for *War Is Kind.* Draft E is evidently an early version of the poem which was considerably revised for the appearance in *The Black Riders.* In preparing the typescript of *War Is Kind,* Crane apparently went back to Draft E (rather than to the version in *The Black Riders*) and re-revised the poem afresh. (It is quite possible that he had forgotten that this poem had appeared in the earlier volume.) The missing typescript—the readings of which only can be inferred from the appearance in Publication 24—is obviously the final revision, and is therefore the authoritative version.

*34*

| | |
|---|---|
| *Versions* | ' 1, 2, 7, 17, 29, 30, 32. |
| *Text* | |
| 3. | ... peddlers. ] 30, 32. |
| 5. | ... SAYING, ] 1, 2, 7, 17. ... saying, ] 29, 30, 32. |
| 8. | ... SAID, "HENCE! ] 1, 2, 7, 17. ... said, "Hence! ] 29, 30, 32. |
| 12. | ... Gods ] 29. |

*35*

| | |
|---|---|
| *Versions* | 1, 2, 7, 17, 29, 30, 32. |
| *Text* | |
| 11. | Ay, ] 30, 32. ... Heavens, ] 29. |

*36*

| | |
|---|---|
| *Versions* | 1, 2, 7, 17, 29, 30, 32. |
| *Text* | |
| 11. | Ay, ] 30, 32. |

*37*

| | |
|---|---|
| *Versions* | 1, 2, 7, 17, 29, 30, 32. |
| *Text* | |
| 4. | ...SANG, ] 1, 2, 7, 17. ...sang, ] 29, 30, 32. |
| 5. | "Ay! we ...we ] 30, 32. |

*38*

| | |
|---|---|
| *Versions* | 1, 2, 7, 17, 29, 30, 32. |
| *Text* | |
| 1. | ...ONCE, ] 1, 2, 7, 17. ...once, ] 29, 30, 32. |
| 6. | ...this— ] 30, 32. |
| 13. | ...more— ] 30, 32. |

*39*

| | |
|---|---|
| *Versions* | 1, 2, 7, 17, 29, 30, 32. |
| *Text* | |
| 4. | ...hearken! ] 30, 32. |

*40*

| | |
|---|---|
| *Versions* | 1, 2, 7, 17, 29, 30, 32. |
| *Text* | |
| 1. | ...ME ] 1, 2, 7, 17. ...me. ] 30, 32. |
| 4. | Ay; ] 30, 32. |
| 10. | ...veil— ] 30, 32. |
| 24. | Ay; ] 30, 32. |

*41*

| | |
|---|---|
| *Versions* | 1, 2, 7, 17, 29, 30, 32. |
| *Text* | |
| 6. | ...heart's pain. ] 30, 32. |

*42*

*Versions*    1, 2, 7, 17, 29, 30, 32.
    *Text*

2.    . . . CRIED, ] 1, 2, 7, 17. . . . cried, ] 29, 30, 32.

4.    . . . SAID, "IT ] 1, 2, 7, 17. . . . said, "It ] 29, 30, 32.

5.    . . . CRIED, "WELL, ] 1, 2, 7, 17. . . . cried, "Well, ] 29, 30, 32.

7.    . . . SAID, "IT ] 1, 2, 7, 17. . . . said, "It ] 29, 30, 32.

*43*

*Versions*    1, 2, 7, 17, 29, 30, 32.
    *Text*

2.    "Good bye! Good bye!" ] 29. . . . good-bye!" ] 30, 32.

4.    "Good bye! Good bye!" ] 29. . . . good-bye!" ] 30, 32.

8.    "Good bye! Good bye!" ] 29. . . . good-bye!" ] 30, 32.

10.    "Good bye! Good bye!" ] 29. . . . good-bye!" ] 30, 32.

*44*

*Versions*    1, 2, 7, 17, 29, 30, 32.

*45*

*Versions*    1, 2, 7, 17, 29, 30, 32.

*46*

*Versions*    1, 2, 7, 17, 29, 30, 32.

*Notes*

    *Text*
    2.     . . . PAGE, ] 1, 2, 7, 17. . . . page, ] 29.

The comma supplied by Copeland & Day is syntactically impossible and must be rejected.

## 47

    *Versions*      1, 2, 7, 17, 29, 30, 32.
    *Text*
    5.     . . . SAID, "I ] 1, 2, 7, 17. . . . said, "I ] 29, 30, 32.

## 48

    *Versions*      1, 2, 7, 17, 29, 30, 32.
    *Text*
    1.     . . . man— ] 30, 32.
    8.     . . . nothing— ] 30, 32.
    11.     . . . pain— ] 30, 32.

## 49

    *Versions*      1, 2, 7, 17, 29, 30, 32.
    *Text*
    7.     . . . THEM, ] 1, 2, 7, 17. . . . them, ] 29, 30, 32.
    8.     . . . what ] 30, 32.
    11.     . . . look! ] 30, 32.
    14.     . . . divine— ] 30, 32.
    22.     . . . look! ] 30, 32.
    34.     . . . DESPAIR, ] 1, 2, 7, 17. . . . despair, ] 29, 30, 32.
    37.     . . . look! ] 30, 32.
    37-38.     [*No break*] ] 29.

39.     . . . SCREAMED, ] 1, 2, 7, 17. . . . screamed, ] 29, 30, 32.
40.     . . . fool! fool! ] 30, 32.

*50*

*Versions*     1, 2, 7, 17, 29, 30, 32.
*Text*
4.     Ay, ] 30, 32.

*51*

*Versions*     1, 2, 7, 17, 29, 30, 32.
*Text*

1.     . . . God— ] 30, 32.
2.     . . . God ] 30, 32.
3.     . . . Deity ] 30, 32.
4.     . . . PUFFING, ] 1, 2, 7, 17. . . . puffing, ] 29, 30, 32.
7.     . . . My Particularly Sublime Majesty." ] 30, 32.
9.     . . . God— ] 30, 32.
10.     . . . God ] 30, 32.
14.     . . . SAID, "MY ] 1, 2, 7, 17. . . . said, "My ] 29, 30, 32.

*52*

*Versions*     1, 2, 7, 17, 29, 30, 32.
*Text*
4.     . . . lord, ] 29.
7.     . . . Thy ] 30, 32.

*53*

*Versions*     1, 2, 7, 17, 29, 30, 32.

*Notes*

> *Text*
>
> | | |
> |---|---|
> | 1. | . . . God, ] 30, 32. |
> | 4. | . . . You ] 30, 32. |
> | 5. | . . . Your ] 30, 32. |
> | 6. | . . . Your ] 30, 32. |
> | 7. | . . . You ] 30, 32. |
> | 10. | . . . You ] 30, 32. |
> | 11. | . . . Thou ] 30, 32. |
> | 12. | . . . Thee ] 30, 32. |
> | 13. | . . . Thee ] 30, 32. |
> | 15. | . . . Thou, . . . Thy ] 30, 32. |
> | 16. | . . . Thy ] 30, 32. |
> | 17. | . . . One ] 30, 32. |
> | 19. | . . . Friend, ] 29. . . . He . . . God; ] 30, 32. |
> | 20. | . . . Him. ] 30, 32. |

## 54

*Versions*   1, 2, 7, 17, 29, 30, 32.

## 55

*Versions*   1, 2, 7, 17, 29, 30, 32.

*Text*

| | |
|---|---|
| 5. | . . . RAGE, ] 1, 2, 7, 17. . . . rage, ] 29, 30, 32. |
| 6. | . . . Do ] 29. |

## 56

*Versions*   1, 2, 7, 17, 29, 30, 32.

## 57

*Versions*   1, 2, 7, 17, 29, 30, 32.

*58*

    *Versions*       1, 2, 7, 17, 29, 30, 32.

*59*

    *Versions*       1, 2, 7, 17, 29, 30, 32.
    *Text*
      7.       . . . Spirit ] 30, 32.

*60*

    *Versions*       1, 2, 7, 17, 29, 30, 32.
    *Text*
      8.       . . . ANXIOUSLY, ] 1, 2, 7, 17. . . . anxiously, ] 29, 30, 32.
      9.       . . . good deed, ] 30, 32.
     15.       . . . vanity. ] 30, 32.
     18.       . . . MYSELF, ] 1, 2, 7, 17. . . . myself. ] 29, 30, 32.

*61*

    *Versions*       1, 2, 7, 17, 29, 30, 32.
    *Text*
      5.       . . . GAILY. ] 7, 17.
     11.       . . . SCREAMING, "FOOL!" ] 1, 2, 7, 17. . . . screaming, "Fool!" ] 29, 30, 32.

*62*

    *Versions*       1, 2, 7, 17, 29, 30, 32.

*63*

    *Versions*       1, 2, 7, 17, 29, 30, 32.

*64*

| *Versions* | 1, 2, 7, 17, 29, 30, 32. |
|---|---|
| *Text* | |
| 8. | . . . FRIEND? ] 1, 2. . . . friend ] 29. |

*65*

| *Versions* | 1, 2, 7, 17, 27, 29, 30, 32. |
|---|---|
| *Text* | [*Title*] 'SCAPED ] 27. |
| 6. | . . . They ] 29. |
| 7. | . . . CRIED, "COME ] 1, 2, 7, 17. . . . cried, "Come ] 27, 29, 30, 32. . . . back, Little Thoughts!" ] 27. |

*66*

| *Versions* | 1, 2, 7, 17, 29, 30, 32. |
|---|---|
| *Text* | |
| 5. | . . . ignorant— ] 30, 32. |

*67*

| *Versions* | 1, 2, 7, 17, 29, 30, 32. |
|---|---|
| *Text* | |
| 1. | . . . heaven; ] 30, 32. |
| 15. | . . . sad— ] 30, 32. |

*68*

| *Versions* | 1, 2, 7, 17, 29, 30, 32. |
|---|---|
| *Text* | |
| 3. | . . . CALLED, ] 1, 2, 7, 17. . . . called, ] 29, 30, 32. |
| 7. | . . . CALLING, ] 1, 2, 7, 17. . . . calling, ] 29, 30, 32. |

14.  ... CALLING, ] 1, 2, 7, 17. ... calling, ] 29, 30, 32.

17.  ... DENIAL, ] 1, 2, 7, 17. ... denial, ] 29, 30, 32.

18-19.  [*Break*] ] 29.

## UNCOLLECTED POEMS

"LEGENDS"

While Williams and Starrett, *Stephen Crane: A Bibliography*, p. 72, suggests that this group of five poems was "intended for publication in *The Black Riders*," there is no evidence to support such a conclusion. There are, in fact, no contemporary documents for the text of the poems other than Publication 14, nor is there any reference to the group in the surviving letters of Crane. (See also the note to *9*, above.) Two reprintings of the group are of interest (although without authority) : In 1942, Williams and Starrett issued *Legends by Stephen Crane,* "Privately printed [by Edwin B. Hill], April, 1942, at Ysleta, Texas, in an edition of only forty-five copies" for their friends; the group also is included in Hoffman, *The Poetry of Stephen Crane,* pp. 281-82. Both versions differ from this edition in the lining of the poems.

*69-73*

*Versions*  14.

*74*

*Versions*  F, 21, 23, 30, 32.
*Text*  [*Title*] THE BLUE BATTALIONS. | STEPHEN CRANE. ] 23.
1.  ... hill, ] 30, 32.

3.    ... tongues and lengthens ] 21, 23, 30, 32. ... arms, ] 23.

5.    ... will [*cancelled*] shall [*substituted*] be ] F.

6.    ... rise, ] 21, 23, 30, 32.

7.    Blue battalions. ] 21, 23, 30, 32.

10.    ... battalions, ] 21, 23, 30, 32.

11.    The blue battalions. ] 21, 23, 30, 32.

12.    ... deep. ] 21, 30, 32. ... deep, ] 23.

13.    ... together. ] 21, 30, 32. ... together, ] 23.

14.    ... looms [*cancelled*] will come [*substituted*] at ... blind, [*cancelled*] eyeless [*substituted*] ] F. ... eyeless. ] 21.

15.    ...beckon, ] 21, 23, 30, 32.

16.    . . . right [*cancelled*] creed [*substituted*] like ... censor ] F.

17.    March the new [*cancelled*] At the head of the new [*substituted*] battalions ] F. . . . battalions, ] 21, 23, 30, 32.

18.    Blue battalions. ] 21, 23, 30, 32.

19.    ... impulse, ] 21, 23, 30, 32.

20.    ... right, ] 21, 23, 30, 32.

21.    ... battalions, ] 21, 30, 32. ... battalion, ] 23.

22.    The blue battalions. ] 21, 23, 30, 32. ... Blue [*capital subsequently altered*] battalions— ] F.

23.    ... crang ] F. ... thy wisdom, ] 21, 23. ... wisdom, ] 30, 32.

24.    ... thy Son's, ] 21, 23. ... Son's; ] 30, 32.

25.    ... ma [*cancelled*] feet [*substituted*] of ] F. ... part— ] 21, 23, 30, 32.

26.      Ay, ] 30, 32. . . . and [*cancelled*] another is [*substituted*] the ] F. . . . youth. ] 21, 23, 30, 32.

27.      Then, swift ] 21, 23, 30, 32. . . . toward [*cancelled*] through a shadow, [*substituted*] ] F. . . . thro ] 21. . . . thro' ] 23.

28.      God, lead the new battalions [*cancelled*] The men of the new battalions [*substituted*] ] F. . . . battalions, ] 21, 23, 30, 32.

29.      Blue battalions. ] 21, 23. Blue ] 30, 32.

30.      . . . the new battalions [*cancelled*] them high. God lead them far [*substituted*] ] F. . . . high, God . . . far, ] 21, 23, 30, 32.

31.      God lead . . . God lead ] 21, 23, 30, 32. . . . high, ] 23, 30, 32.

32.      . . . battalions, ] 21, 23, 30, 32.

33.      The blue battalions. ] 21, 23, 30, 32.

Draft F is undoubtedly the source for the *Philistine* appearance of the poem, Publication 21. While it is quite possible that Crane thoroughly revised the poem in the fair copy from which Publication 21 was prepared, the variations from the original text in that appearance seem to violate throughly the intent of the poem. For example, "thro" in publication 21 (line 27) is a product of Elbert Hubbard's program of simplified spelling. This was further sophisticated by the editor of publication 23 who inserted the apostrophe. For that reason, the text of Draft F has been returned to as the source of this poem. "Crang" (line 23) appears at first glance to be a portmanteau word formed by the blending of "crash" and "clang." But nowhere else does Crane adopt this technique; the slight space between the second and third letters of the word in Draft F suggests that Crane began to write "crash," and then changed his mind and continued the word as "clang."

The substitution of "censer" for "censor" in Publication 21, however, is undoubtedly correct, and Draft F probably records a misspelling. As the son of a Methodist minister at the time of a formalistic revival, Crane could not have escaped being impressed with the emotional and symbolic impact of the censer being swung to distribute its incense.

Publication 23 derived directly from Elbert Hubbard's version of the poem in Publication 21. The signed appearance in a popular anthology that was sold at $2.50, is a mark of popular recognition of sorts. The Follett collections, Publications 30 and 32, also derived from Publication 21. In both of the collected editions of the poems, *74* is placed in *War Is Kind,* immediately preceding the "Intrigue" poems. This position is misleading and completely unauthorized.

*75*

*Versions*     22.

## WAR IS KIND

As in the first volume of poetry, the title of this collection derives from the first poem in the volume. But one edition of the book (Publication 24) was issued during Crane's lifetime. Two editions listed in the literature cannot be traced: Stolper, *Stephen Crane: A List of His Writings,* p. 16, records a 1900 edition published in New York (which is probably an erroneous recording of Publication 24) ; Williams and Starrett, *Stephen Crane: A Bibliography,* pp. 41, 130, notes that "Later editions of this title are in a smaller format. A 'New Edition' is dated [New York: Frederick A. Stokes Company] 1902"

(this is repeated from the comment in Starrett's *Stephen Crane: A Bibliography*, p. 28.)

*76*

Since Draft H appears above the year "1895" on a preliminary leaf of a copy of *The Red Badge* of Courage presented to William Dean Howells, and since Crane dated another inscription in the book as "August 17, 1895," it would appear to be reasonable to suppose that *76* was written in the first half of 1895. But the copy in which these inscriptions appear is the 1896 Appleton issue, a volume which could not have been available two months before the date of publication of the first edition. In this case, Crane's misdating must be considered intentional, a way of backdating his expression of gratitude to Howells. (It is quite conceivable, incidentally, that the book was presented to Howells as a New Year's gift. On 26 January 1896 Howells thanked Crane for his New Year's greeting, and went on to comment that while he was pleased by the success in England of *The Red Badge,* he thought *Maggie* better than that book and *The Black Riders.* See Stallman and Gilkes, *Letters,* p. 102.)

| | |
|---|---|
| *Versions* | G, H, I, 9, 24, 30, 32. |
| *Text* | [*Title*] WAR IS KIND. ] I, 9, 24. |
| 1. | . . . kind ] H. |
| 3. | . . . alone ] H. |
| 6. | Hoarse booming . . . regiment ] G, H. |
| 7. | . . . fight ] G, H. |
| 8. | . . . die ] G, H. |
| 9. | . . . them ] G, H. |
| 10. | . . . battle-god, . . . kingdom— ] G, H, 9, 24, 30, 32. |
| 11. | . . . —A ] H. . . . place [*cancelled*] field [*substituted*] where ] G. |

12.    ... kind ] H, I.
13.    ... trenches ] H.
14.    ... died ] H.
15.    ... weep ] H.
16.    ... kind ] H.
17.    ... regiment ] H.
18.    ... gold ] H.
19.    ... die ] H. ... die, ] I.
20.    ... slaughter ] H.
22.    ... lie ] H.
24.    ... son ] H.
25.    ... weep ] H.

Draft G contains only lines 6-11. It and Draft H are undoubtedly fair copies; Draft H even precedes the first four lines with opening quotation marks. Publication 9 appears in large and small capital letters.

## 77

Draft K, a fair copy dated 28 December 1895, suggests that the poem was written before this date. (The Dr. A. L. Mitchell to whom Draft K was presented was the advertiser in the *Philistine*, IX, 1 (June 1899), [vii]: "—DR. A. L. MITCHELL—Physician and Surgeon. TREPANNING A SPECIALTY. OFFICE NEXT DOOR TO THE PHILISTINE EAST AURORA, N. Y.") Since the first publication of 77 was in the February, 1896, *Philistine* (Publication 10), that circumstance does not appear to be unreasonable.

*Versions*    J, K, L, 10, 13, 24, 30, 32.
   *Text*    [*Title*] The Shell and the Pines [*cancelled*] ] J.
   3.    ... us ] J, K.

4.      . . . ships ] J, K.

5.      . . . ships". ] L.

6.      . . . seas [*final* s *cancelled*] ] K. . . . oh, pines
        ] J, K. . . . O, Pines, ] L. . . . O Pines, ] 24,
        30, 32.

8.      . . . doom ] J, K.

10.     . . . tears ] J, K. . . . tears. ] 10.

11.     . . robes ] J, K.

12.     —Men ] J, K.

13.     . . . pain". ] L.

16.     . . . us ] J, K.

17.     . . . ships ] K.

19.     . . . oh, pines ] J, K. . . . O, Pines ] L. . . . O
        Pines, ] 24, 30, 32.

20.     . . . moonlight ] J, K. . . . moonlight; ] 24,
        30, 32.

21.     . . . patience ] J, K.

22.     . . . hands ] J, K.

23.     . . . hearts ] J, K. . . . hearts. ] 10.
        . . . HEARTS. ] 13.

24.     . . . seas [*final* s *cancelled*] ] K. . . . O, Pines".
        ] L. . . . O Pines." ] 24, 30, 32.

27.     . . . us ] J, K.

28.     . . . ships ] J, K.

29.     . . . ships". ] L.

30.     . . . oh, pines ] J, K. . . . O, Pines, ] L. . . . O
        Pines, ] 24, 30, 32.

31.     . . . sea ] J, K.

32.     . . . you ] J, K.

33.     . . . ships ] J, K.

34.     O puny ] L, 24, 30, 32. . . . pines". ] L.

*Notes*

Draft J, the manuscript, is the earliest state of the poem, and one of the few surviving manuscripts that show signs of having passed through the hands of a printer. Directly or indirectly this draft was the source of Publication 10, which was in turn the source of another Elbert Hubbard venture, Publication 13. (Publication 13 is printed entirely in capital letters.)

*78*

| *Versions* | M, 12, 13, 24, 30, 32. |
| --- | --- |
| *Text* | |
| 2. | . . . meadow, ] 24, 30, 32. |
| 7. | . . . vacancy, ] 24, 30, 32. |
| 8. | . . . time, ] 24, 30, 32. . . . TIME, ] 13. |

Publications 12 and 13 are printed entirely in capital letters.

*79*

Elbert Hubbard precedes the reproduction of Draft N in the *Fra,* July 1900, p. xxv, with a statement that provides the possibility for distorting the dating of the poem: "A few weeks before his passing, Stevie Crane sent me this manuscript. I thought it tipped too much to t'other side when I first read it. But I got it out the other day and read it again. I liked it better. THE FRA readers shall judge." But since the final version of *79* appeared in *War Is Kind,* Hubbard would have had to have received the early draft well before Crane's death in June, 1900. (See also Crane's note to Hubbard on Draft N, p. 158, above.)

| *Versions* | N, O, 24, 30, 32. |
| --- | --- |
| *Text* | |
| 2. | . . . cant ] O. |
| 10. | . . . numskulls? ] 24, 30, 32. |

12.      . . . upon [*inserted subsequently*] the . . . pul-
piting ] N.

Draft N consists of lines 7-19 only, but it undoubtedly
represents the complete poem as it existed at that time.

## 80

Versions      P, 24, 30, 32.
   Text
   3.       . . . dead, ] 24, 30, 32.
   5.       . . . listen! ] 30, 32.
   6.       . . . thud of ] 24, 30, 32.

## 81

The legal cap paper on which Draft Q is written suggests
that this poem was written quite early in Crane's career. In
1947, Melvin Schoberlin supplied the lining to a letter from
Crane to Cora Stewart (Stallman and Gilkes, *Letters*, p. 138,
dates the letter as January, 1897) and printed it as *Lines By
Stephen Crane* (Baltimore: The Mogollon Press, 1947) with
the implication that this was an "original draft" of *81*. (See
below for the letter and Schoberlin's text.) But since Crane
almost certainly wrote Draft Q before he left for Florida in
November, 1896, it is more probable that he based the letter
to Cora on his recollection of the poem, rather than that the
poem was based on the letter. If this is true, the letter explains
more about his procedure in courting than it does about his
poetic process. (See also the note to *126*.)

Versions      Q, R, S, 16, 24, 27, 30, 32.
   Text       [*Title*] LINES. ] 16.
   1.         I [*added subsequently*] Explain ] Q. . . . path
              . . . night ] Q,S. . . . PATH ] 16.

2.      . . . WAVE, ] 16. . . . wave, ] 24, 27, 30, 32.

3.      . . . STRIVING, ] 16. . . . striving, ] 24, 27, 30, 32.

4.      . . . MAN, ] 16. . . . man, ] 24, 27, 30, 32.

5.      Then [*cancelled*] The [T *capitalized subsequently*] shadow ] Q. The ] S. . . . NIGHT, ] 16. . . . night, ] 24, 27, 30, 32.

6.      . . . star; ] 24, 27, 30, 32.

6-7.    Then, the silence [*cancelled*] ] Q. [*No break*] ] 30, 32.

7.      . . . waste waters ] Q,S. . . . waters, ] 24, 27, 30, 32.

8.      . . . waves. ] Q, S.

·9.     . . . lonliness. ] Q, R.

9-10.   Explain [*cancelled*] | Oh, thou, my ship ] Q. Oh, thou, my ship ] S.

10.     . . . thou, in thy stern straight journey ] Q, S. . . . LOVE ! ] 16. . . . love, ] 24, 27, 30, 32.

11.     . . . leavest a waste, a waste of far waters ] Q, S. . . . waters, ] 24, 27, 30, 32.

12.     . . . waters [*cancelled*] waves [*substituted*] ] Q.

13.     . . . lonliness. ] Q, R.


Draft Q appears to be the original manuscript of the poem. Publication 16 was probably prepared from a fair copy which incorporated many revisions, while Draft R—the *War Is Kind* typescript copy—went back to Q and revised in another direction. On Crane's death, Cora prepared a copy of this poem for an edition which she submitted to the periodicals. In it, she returned to Q and abided by Crane's own corrections embodied in that manuscript.

Melvin Schoberlin's *Lines by Stephen Crane* is based on

Stephen Crane to Cora Ethel Stewart (later Cora Crane), in Stallman and Gilkes, *Letters*, p. 138:

> Love comes like the tall swift shadow of a ship at night. There is for a moment, the music of the water's turmoil, a bell, perhaps, a man's shout, a row of gleaming yellow lights. Then the slow sinking of this mystic shape. Then silence and a bitter silence—the silence of the sea at night.

Schoberlin's adaption provided new lining, and occasionally changed the punctuation:

> Love comes like a tall, swift shadow of a ship at night.
> There is for a moment,
> The music of the water's turmoil,
> A bell,
> Perhaps a man's shout,
> A row of gleaming yellow lights;
> Then the slow sinking of this mystic shape.
>
> Then the silence,
> And a bitter silence—
> The silence of the sea at night.

The Schoberlin printing cannot, of course, be ascribed any authority in determining the text of the poem.

Publication 16 was printed entirely in capital letters.

82

| | |
|---|---|
| *Versions* | T, 5, 8, 13, 24, 30, 32. |
| *Text* | |
| 1. | ...birches, ] 24, 30, 32. |
| 2. | ...White ] T. ...SILENCE. ] 5, 8, 13. |
| | ...silence, ] 24, 30, 32. |
| 4. | ...NIGHTFALL, ] 5, 8, 13. |

6.      ... WIND-MEN. ] 5, 8, 13.
7.      ... MANIAC, ] 5, 8, 13.
9.      But you— ] 24, 30, 32.
10.     ... roses." ] T.

Publications 5, 8, and 13 are printed entirely in capital letters.

## 83

*Versions*      U, V, 13, 15, 24, 30, 32.
  *Text*
1.      ... knight— ] U.
2.      ... reeking, ] 24, 30, 32.
3.      ... sword, ] 24, 30, 32.
5.      ... knight, ] 24, 30, 32.
7.      ... steel flicked ] U.
8.      ... lights, ] 24, 30, 32.
9.      ... KNIGHTS ] 13. ... GOOD KNIGHT'S BANNER ] 15.
11.     ... horse, ] 24, 30, 32.
12.     ... thing, ] 24, 30, 32.
13.     ... of a castle ] U.
15.     ... of a castle ] U.

Publications 13 and 15 are printed entirely in capital letters.

## 84

*Versions*      W, X, 24, 30, 32.
  *Text*
3.      ... him, he ... in far unknown ] W.
6.      Flashing yellow ] W.
7.      ... bystander ] W, X.

8-9.     And when his [*cancelled*] ] W.

9.     . . . man in a passion ] W. . . . man. ] 24, 30, 32.

10.     . . . his cane ] W.

11.     It had become two canes. ] W.

## 85

*Versions*     Y, 19, 24, 30, 32.

*Text*

2.     . . . YOU IT ] 19.

3.     . . . candle, and ] 30, 32.

Publication 19 is printed entirely in capital letters.

## 86

*Versions*     Z, A$^1$, B$^1$, 20, 24, 30, 32.

*Text*     [*Title*] Lines [*in an unidentified hand*] ] Z. LINES. ] A$^1$, 20.

3.     Fire rays ] 24, 30, 32.

7.     . . . distant thunder ] 30, 32. . . . drums, ] 24, 30, 32.

8.     While mystic ] Z, B, 20, 24, 30, 32. . . . mystic [*on printed page, cancelled*] slow [*substituted*] things ] A$^1$. . . . color, ] 24. . . . colour, ] 30, 32.

12.     . . . snakes, ] 24, 30, 32.

13.     . . . staring, ] 24, 30, 32.

18.     On [*superscribed into* Over *and then cancelled*] Over [*inserted*] the ] Z.

21.     . . . her, ] 24, 30, 32.

29.     . . . death, ] 24, 30, 32.

Draft Z was the source of Publication 20, proof for which—Draft A$^1$—was requested by Crane, was corrected by him, and was never returned to the *Philistine*. The return to "mystic" in Draft B¹ (line 8) may have been a reconsideration by Crane. But it is more likely that "slow" was preferred, was never sent, and was overlooked in the haste of preparing the typescript from the unrevised appearance in Publication 20.

## 87

| | |
|---|---|
| *Versions* | 24, 30, 32. |
| *Text* | |
| 17. | . . . is feckless ] 30, 32. |

Crane characteristically used "fetless," as in "Memoirs of a Private": ". . . a doddering fetless old man." Reprinted in Stallman and Hagemann, *War Dispatches*, p. 213.

## 88

| | |
|---|---|
| *Versions* | C¹, 24, 27, 30, 32. |
| *Text* | [*Title*] THE WAYFARER ] 27. |
| 1. | . . . wayfarer, ] 24, 27, 30, 32. |
| 2. | . . . truth, ] 24, 37, 30, 32. |
| 5. | "Ha," ] C¹. |
| 7. | . . . time." ] C¹. |
| 10. | "Well," ] C¹. |
| 11. | . . . roads." ] C¹. |

## 89

| | |
|---|---|
| *Versions* | D¹, 6, 13, 24, 30, 32. |
| *Text* | |
| 1. | . . . walls, ] 24, 30, 32. |
| 2-3. | [*No break*] ] D¹. |
| 3. | . . . hymn, ] 24, 30, 32. |
| 4. | . . . OF CLASHES AND CRIES, ] 13. . . . CRIES, ] 6. . . . cries, ] 24, 30, 32. |

9.    . . . OF VIOLETS, ] 6, 13. . . . flowers, ] 24, 30, 32.

13.   "O, ] D¹, 13. "OH GOD SAVE US!" ] 6. . . . US! ] 13. "O God, save us!" ] 24, 30, 32.

Publications 6 and 13 are printed entirely in capital letters.

## 90

This poem probably was written before early 1897. Dating is by means of the scrawled "The name of this club shall be the Hartwood Club" which appears upside-down at the bottom of Draft E¹. Hartwood is a small town in Sullivan County, New York, not far from Monticello, New York. On 11 February 1896, Crane wrote Nellie Crouse that "In Hartwood I have a great chance to study the new-rich. The Hartwood Clubhouse is only three miles away and there are some of the new rich in it." (See Stallman and Gilkes, *Letters*, p. 115.) Crane had probably gained access to the Club through the offices of his brother, Judge William Crane of Hartwood.

*Versions*   E¹, F¹, 24, 30, 32.
  *Text*

1.    Once a man clambering . . . house-tops ] 24. Once a man clambering . . . housetops ] 30, 32

2.    Cried there to the imperturbab ] E¹. . . . the empty heavens ] F¹.

3.    . . . voice he [*added subsequently*] called . . . the imperturbable stars ] F¹.

4.    . . . the higher suns. ] F¹.

5.    . . . was an indication, a dot, ] F¹.

6+7.  Then, finally—God—the sky was filled with armies ] F¹.

Draft E¹ offers an interesting insight into Crane's poetic

workshop since it consists of what must be the earliest state of any poem; E¹ consists of only two lines and the word "Once" scrawled again below the second line.

## 91

| | |
|---|---|
| *Versions* | G¹ , 24, 30, 32. |
| *Text* | |
| 2. | . . . sing ] G¹. |
| 3. | . . . lamentable. ] 24, 30, 32. |
| 5. | And in the clip-clapper \| Of this tongue of wood ] G¹. |
| 6. | He understood ] G¹. |
| 7. | What the man wished to sing ] G¹. |
| 8. | And with this \| The singer was well satisfied. ] G¹. |

Draft G¹ is reprinted with occasional errors of transcription in Hoffman, *The Poetry of Stephen Crane,* p. 20. This draft is probably the version originally submitted to Copeland and Day as part of the manuscript of *The Black Riders and Other Lines* (see p. xxviii). It was the fourth poem on the list of poems that Copeland and Day wished omitted from the volume.

## 92

According to the date at the bottom of Draft H¹, the poem was composed on "Dec 5th, 1897."

| | |
|---|---|
| *Versions* | H¹, I¹, 24, 30, 32. |
| *Text* | |
| 1+2 | The successful man has thrust himself through the paper [*cancelled*] water [*substituted*] of the years ] H¹. |

3.        . . . mistakes; ] I¹. . . . mistakes,— ] 24. . . . mistakes— ] 30, 32.

3+4.      Reeking wet with mistakes, bloody mistakes, ] H¹.

5.        . . . lesser, ] 24, 30, 32.

7.        With the bones of fools ] H¹.

8+9.      He buys silken banners bearing [*cancelled*] limned with [*substituted*] his triumphant face ] H¹.

9.        . . . face; ] 24, 30, 32.

11.       . . . all ] H¹.

12+13.    Flesh and marrow contribute a coverlet ] H¹.

13.       . . . coverlet, ] 24, 30, 32.

14.       . . . slumber ] H¹.

15.       . . . ignorance; in ] H¹. . . . guilt, ] 24, 30, 32.

18.       . . . smiling ] I¹.

21.       . . . babes ] H¹.

21-22.    Protests his murder of widows. ] H¹.

22.       . . . dripping ] I¹.


*93*

*Versions*   J¹, K¹, L¹, 11, 24, 27, 30, 32.

*Text*       [*Title*] VERSES [*cancelled*] ] K¹. [*Title*] VERSES ] 11. [*Title*] THE PEAKS ] 27.

2.        Grey heavy ] J¹, L¹, 24, 30, 32. . . . valleys ] J¹, L¹.

3.        . . . God alone. ] L¹, 24, 27, 30, 32.

4.        . . . master, that moveth . . . finger ] J¹. "O Master, that ] K¹, 11, 24, 27, 30, 32. "O, Master . . . finger ] L¹.

5.        Humble idle futile ] L¹.

6.     . . . world ] K¹, 11.
7.     . . . thy ] J¹, L¹. . . . feet. ] L.¹
9.     . . . miles, ] K¹, 11, 24, 37, 30, 32.
11.     "O Master, that ] K¹, 11, 24, 27, 30, 32. "O, Master ] L¹. . . . knoweth [*last two letters cancelled*] knowest [*substituted*] the wherefore . . . rain-drops ] J¹. . . . the wherefore [*cancelled*] meaning [*substituted*] ] K¹. . . . rain-drops, ] 27, 30, 32.
13.     Grant [*cancelled*] Give [*substituted*] voice . . . us we pray oh Lord ] J¹.
14.     . . . may chant thy ] J¹. . . . may chant [*cancelled*] sing [*substituted*] Thy ] K¹. . . . sun". ] L¹.
16-17.     [*Break*] ] J¹.
17.     . . . master ] J¹. "O Master, ] K¹, 11, 24, 27, 30, 32. "O, Master, ] L¹.
18.     Thou that ] L¹, 24, 27, 30, 32. . . . and swallows ] J¹. . . . and swallows, [*cancelled*] birds [*substituted*] ] K¹.
20.     Thou alone needeth [*cancelled*] only, needest [*substituted*] eternal patience ] J¹.
21.     . . . thy . . . oh, Lord— ] J¹.
22.     . . . peaks". ] L¹.
24.     Grey heavy ] J¹, L¹, 24, 30, 32. . . . valleys, ] K¹, 11, 24, 27, 30, 32.
25.     . . . God alone. ] L¹, 24, 27, 30, 32.

Draft J¹, the original manuscript, probably was the source of Publication 11, a corrected page of which formed Draft K¹. From Draft K¹ came Draft L¹, the typescript for *War is Kind*. Maurice Bassan's "A Bibliographical Study of Stephen Crane's Poem, 'In the Night'," *PSBA,* LVIII (Second Quarter, 1964) , 173-179 (the first attempt at providing a critical text of *any* of Crane's poems) decided on Draft K[1] as the final text of the poem. In so doing, he rejected Publication 24 (and, of course, all versions after that) because there is no evidence of Crane's participation in that text, and he rejected L[1] (Bassan's state 6) since he believed that it showed no evidence of Crane's hand. But an analysis of all of the components of the typescript of *War Is Kind* does evidence Crane's hand: there are the misspellings (of which "lonliness" is an example) which Crane perpetrated; the uncertainty in the conventions of grammar and punctuation which led him to adopt readings of the publication immediately preceding his final draft; the novice's error in placing punctuation outside quotation marks when typing a text; and the error at the beginning of *103*, line 45 in Draft Z[1], which was transferred to Publication 24. (Crane had asked Hamlin Garland to help him rescue a manuscript of *The Red Badge of Courage* from the "typewriter," and—on 2 March 1899—Crane apologised to his brother William about his deficiencies as a correspondent and promised a remedy: "Since we have had this machine [a typewriter] I have lost some of my habits of being an ill correspondent." (See William White, "A Stephen Crane Letter," *Times* (London) *Literary Supplement,* 22 September 1961.) Crane was therefore one of the first authors to rely on the typewriter; more importantly, it helps date the typescript copy of *War Is Kind* in early 1899 (certainly before March, probably after January) . Since Crane's hand is quite evident in the typescript for *War Is Kind,* Draft K[1] must be rejected in favor of Draft L[1] as Crane's final text of the poem.

*94*

*Versions*     M[1], 3, 12, 24, 30, 32.

> *Text*
>
> 7.     . . . PADDLE, ] 3, 13. . . . paddle, ] 24, 30, 32.
>
> 8.     . . . SOFT, SEARCHING ] 3, 13.
>
> 10-11.     LIFT YOUR GREY FACE! ] 3, 13.

Publications 3 and 13 are printed entirely in capital letters.

*95*

> *Versions*     N¹, 18, 24, 26, 30, 32.
>
> *Text*     [*Title*] SOME THINGS. ] 18.
>
> 2.     . . . WARM AND ] 18. . . . red light ] 26. . . . light, ] 24, 30, 32.
>
> 3.     . . . TABLE ] 18.
>
> 4.     . . . shadows, ] 26.
>
> 5-6.     [*No break*] ] 18.
>
> 8.     . . . flunkeys, ] 24, 30, 32.
>
> 10.     . . . SABRE. ] 18. . . . sabre. ] 24, 26.
>
> 18.     SIMPERED AT BY PIMPLED MER-CHANTS ] 18. Simpered at by pimpled merchants ] 26.
>
> 22.     . . . LIVES. ] 18. . . . lives. ] 26.
>
> 24.     . . . FEET ] 18. . . . feet ] 24, 26, 30, 32.
>
> 25.     . . . BAUBLES ] 18. . . . baubles ] 26.
>
> 26.     Forgetting state, ] N¹.
>
> 27.     . . . HATS, ] 18. . . . hats, ] 24, 30, 32.
>
> 28.     [*Deleted*] ] 26.

Publication 18 is printed entirely in capital letters. The softening of line 18 in this publication is probably Elbert Hubbard's. For Crane's deference to Hubbard's "discretion" see the note to *79*. Publication 26 is printed as part of an article on "Ali Baba," the *Philistine* handyman and an East

Aurora character who fancied hats. This printing was obviously shaped by the requirements of Hubbard's article, and cannot be accorded any authority.

*96*

    *Versions*    24, 30, 32.

*97*

    *Versions*    $0^1$, 24, 30, 32.

    *Text*

        5.    . . . lands, ] 24, 30, 32.

*98*

    *Versions*    24, 27, 30, 32.

    *Text*    [*Title*] THE VIOLETS ] 27.

*99*

This poem was printed in *War Is Kind* in a version revised from the appearance in *The Black Riders and Other Lines;* in this critical edition of Stephen Crane's poetry, the poem appears in its original position and its text is discussed in the note to *33.*

*100*

    *Versions*    $P^1$, 24, 30, 32.

    *Text*

        1.    Ay, ] 30, 32. . . . dream, ] 24, 30, 32.

        4.    Breezes, and ] 24, 30, 32.

*101*

    *Versions*    $Q^1$, 4, 13, 24, 30, 32.

    *Text*

        1.    . . . voice, ] 24, 30, 32.

2.      A ] 24, 30, 32. A latern ] Q¹.

4.      . . . colours ] 30, 32. . . . WATER, ] 4, 13. 13.

5.      . . . LEAF-SHADOWS . . . WAVERED ] 4, 13. . . . leaf-shadow ] 24, 30, 32. . . . wavered ] 24.

6.      . . . HILLS, ] 4, 13. . . . hills, ] 24, 30, 32.

7.      . . . silence, ] 24, 30, 32.

8.      . . . colours ] 30, 32.

9-10.      [*No break*] ] 13.

13.      . . . ETERNITY WITH ] 4, 13.

14.      . . . FATHERS, ] 4, 13. . . . fathers, ] 24, 30, 32.

15.      . . . hymning, ] 24, 30, 32.

16.      . . . WATER, ] 4, 13. . . . water, ] 24, 30, 32.

Publications 4 and 13 are printed entirely in capital letters.

## 102

*Versions*    R¹, 24, 30, 32.
    *Text*

7.      Having ] 24, 30, 32.

23.     The ] 24, 30, 32.

26.     . . . Lord", ] R¹. . . . lord," ] 24, 30, 32.

28.     . . . wisdom". ] R¹. . . . are displaced ] 24, 30, 32.

## "INTRIGUE"

The "Intrigue" cycle was probably written in 1898, while Crane was in Cuba reporting the Spanish-American War. On 20 October, Crane wrote his agent, Paul Revere Reynolds, that "The 'Intrigue' lot goes to Heinemann." (See Stallman and Gilkes, *Letters,* p. 189.)

Crane evidently spent much time in arranging and re-arranging the sequence of the poems in the cycle. On the versos of the twenty-three surviving typescripts of the poems (each typescript contains a stanza of the cycle) are a series of circled numbers that are obviously page numbers denoting one order of the sequence. These numbers are as follows: $S^1 = 1$; $T^1 = 2$; $U^1 = 3$; $V^1 = 4$; $W^1 = 5$; $X^1 = 6$; $Y^1 = 7$; $Z^1 = 8$; $A^2 = 11$; $B^2 = 10$; $C^2 = 12$; $D^2 = 9$; $E^2 = 16$; $F^2 = 17$; $G^2 = 18$; $H^2 = 19$; $I^2 = 14$; $J^2 = 13$; $K^2 = 20$; $L^2 = 21$; $M^2 = 22$; $N^2 = 15$; $O^2 = 23$.

In preparing the typescript of the cycle, Crane recorded a second series of numbers at the foot of the rectos of several poems. This series in is roman numerals, as follows: $E^2 = $ i; $F^2 = $ ii; $G^2 = $ iii; $H^2 = $ iv; $K^2 = $ vii; $L^2 = $ viii; $M^2 = $ ix; $O^2 = $ xi.

This edition follows the sequence of the poems in Publication 24 as indicated by the capitalization of the initial words at the beginning of each group of stanzas. The texts of the poems, however, are reproduced (except for corrections of obvious errors in accidentals) from the last authoritative versions, the typescripts.

*103*

*Versions*  $S^1$, $T^1$, $U^1$, $V^1$, $W^1$, $X^1$, $Y^1$, $Z^1$, $A^2$, $B^2$, $C^2$, $D^2$, 24, 30, 32.

*Text*
1.    . . . love, ] 24, 30, 32.
2.    . . .sundown. ] 24, 30, 32.
3.    . . . soothe, ] 24, 30, 32.
5.    . . . brooks, ] 24, 30, 32.
7.    . . . love, ] 24, 30, 32.
9.    . . . sky, ] 24, 30, 32.
11.    . . . tree, ] 24, 30, 32.

14.    . . . owl— ] 24, 30, 32.
16.    . . . love, ] 24, 30, 32.
17.    . . . thing, ] 24, 30, 32.
19.    . . . easily, ] 24, 30, 32.
21.    . . . sorrow— ] 24, 30, 32.
22.    . . . me. ] 24, 30, 32.
23.    . . . love, ] U¹, 24, 30, 32.
24.    . . . violet, ] 24, 30, 32.
25.    . . . sun-caresses, ] 24, 30, 32.
26.    . . . carelessly— ] 24, 30, 32.
28.    . . . love, ] 24, 30, 32.
29.    . . . love, ] 24, 30, 32.
30.    . . . ashes, ] 24, 30, 32.
31.    . . . them— ] 24, 30, 32.
32.    . . . me. ] 24, 30, 32.
33.    . . . love, ] 24, 30, 32.
35.    . . . face— ] 24, 30, 32.
37.    . . . love, ] 24, 30, 32.
38.    . . . temple, ] 24, 30, 32.
39.    . . . altar, ] 24, 30, 32.
40.    . . . heart— ] 24, 30, 32.
42.    . . . love, ] 24, 30, 32.
44.    . . . thee, ] 24, 30, 32.
45.    From I ] Z¹, 24.
46.    . . . lies— ] 24, 30, 32.
48.    . . . love, ] 24, 30, 32.
49.    . . . priestess, ] 24, 30, 32.
50.    . . . dagger, ] 24, 30, 32.
51.    . . . surely— ] 24, 30, 32.
53.    . . . love, ] 24, 30, 32.
54.    . . . eyes, ] 24, 30, 32.
55.    . . . thee. ] 24, 30, 32.
57.    . . . love, ] 24, 30, 32.

58. . . . thee. ] 24, 30, 32.
60. . . . murder— ] 24, 30, 32.
62. . . . love, ] 24, 30, 32.
63. . . . death, ] 24, 30, 32.
64. Ay, thou ] 30, 32.
65. . . . black, ] 24, 30, 32.
66. . . . thee, ] 24, 30, 32.
67. . . . thee— ] 24, 30, 32.
68. . . . Welcome ] D².

The transference of the orthographical error in line 45 from Draft Z¹ to publication 24 confirms the authority of the drafts and supports the textual hypothesis in the Textual Introduction to *War Is Kind,* and in the note to *93.*

*104*

*Versions* E², F², G², H², I², J², K²,L², 24, 30, 32.
*Text*

1. Love, forgive . . . grief, ] 24, 30, 32.
3. . . . breast, ] 24, 30, 32.
5. . . . grief. ] 24, 30, 32.
7. . . . surrender, ] 24, 30, 32.
8. And thus ] 24, 30. 32.
11. . . . room, ] 24, 30, 32.
12. A suroy ] G². . . . picture, ] 24, 30, 32.
14+15. —Merely a fat complacence of men who know fine women— ] 24, 30, 32.
21. . . . gnash, ] 24, 30, 32.
22. . . . shoe, ] 24, 30, 32.
24. . . . medals, ] 24, 30, 32.
25. . . . honors, ] 24. . . . honours, ] 30, 32.
26. . . . sweetheart, ] 24, 30, 32.
28. The ] 24, 30, 32.
30. . . . love. ] 24, 30, 32.

| | |
|---|---|
| 36. | . . . friends, ] 24, 30, 32. |
| 37. | . . . civil, ] 24, 30, 32. |
| 40. | . . . desire ] 24, 30, 32. |
| 41. | . . . chosen; ] 24, 30, 32. |
| 44. | . . . stride, ] 24, 30, 32. |
| 45. | . . . gesture, ] 24, 30, 32. |
| 48. | . . . intention. ] 24, 30, 32. |

## 105

*Versions*   M², 24, 30, 32.
   *Text*

| | |
|---|---|
| 1. | . . . moved, ] 24, 30, 32. |
| 4. | . . . comb, a ] 24, 30, 32. |
| 5. | Ah, ] 24, 30, 32. |

## 106

*Versions*   N², 24, 30, 32.
   *Text*

| | |
|---|---|
| 4. | . . . happy. ] N². |
| 5. | . . . womanhood, ] 24, 30, 32. |
| 7. | . . . I knew it. ] 24, 30, 32. |
| 8. | . . . miserable, and ] 24, 30, 32. |
| 9. | . . . head, ] 24, 30, 32. |
| 10. | . . . ogre, ] 24, 30, 32. |
| 11. | . . . castle, ] 24, 30, 32. |
| 12. | . . . cruelly, ] 24, 30, 32. |
| 13. | . . . mourning. ] 24, 30, 32. |

## 107

*Versions*   O², 24, 30, 32.
   *Text*

| | |
|---|---|
| 3. | . . . real, ] 24, 30, 32. |

5.　　...dead, ] 24, 30, 32.
6.　　...alive— ] 24, 30, 32.
7.　　A swimish numskull ] O². . . . numskull ]
　　　24, 30, 32.
9.　　...peace! ] 24, 30, 32.

"Numbskull" (spelled thus) is one of Crane's favorite epithets. While it is used quite frequently in his prose, the word appears but twice in the poetry. His more common spelling of the word is recorded in this text. (See also Drafts N and O of *79*, line 10.) "Swimish," also in line 7, has been considered an error.

## *108*

*Versions*　　24, 30, 32.

## *109*

*Versions*　　24, 30, 32.

## *110*

*Versions*　　24, 30, 32.

## *111*

*Versions*　　24, 30, 32.
　*Text*
　　4.　　...glare— ] 30, 32.
　　15.　　...belovèd. ] 30, 32.

## *112*

*Versions*　　24, 30, 32.

## POSTHUMOUSLY PUBLISHED POEMS

The poems in this section are arranged chronologically in order of first publication; within that order the poems are arranged in approximate order of composition. While (contrary to general critical opinion) Crane experimented in verse techniques, the short span of his career as a poet makes unreliable the dating of the manuscripts through charting the progression of the techniques used in the poems. In the six years in which he made a serious commitment to poetry, Crane added to—rather than sustituted within—the range of possibilities he developed for himself.

*113-115* were first published in Publication 31 as "THREE POEMS | *by Stephen Crane.*" (A reproduction of Draft P² preceded the group of poems.) While the group title is not Crane's, and while the group has no integrity other than that resulting from the common first publication, it was reprinted with the title as the last section of Publication 32. The following statement appears on the section half-title in Publication 32 (p. [127]):

> These poems were found in Jacksonville in 1928 among a collection of Stephen Crane's papers which had lain long undisturbed. The manuscripts were given to a friend by the poet's wife, Cora Crane, and remained forgotten until they were discovered by Carl Bohnenberger, Assistant Librarian of the Jacksonville Library. They first appeared in print in the April 1929 issue of The Bookman.

Gilkes, *Cora Crane,* pp. 377-78, discusses the unusual circumstances of Bohnenberger's possession of this material. The collection that Bohnenberger owned now forms the basis of Columbia University's Stephen and Cora Crane Collection.

### 113

*The Poetry of Stephen Crane*, p. 94, suggests that this was written before June, 1898. See also Appendix III.

| | |
|---|---|
| *Versions* | P², Q², 31, 32. |
| Text | |
| 6. | . . . , of of [*cancelled*] and ] P². |
| 12. | . . . are [*cancelled*] may be [*substituted*] turned ] P². |
| 14. | By the [*cancelled*] Because [*substituted*] of . . . child. [*cancelled*] babe [*substituted*] ] P². |
| 14-15. | God is cold. [*cancelled*] ] P². |
| 15. | The seas turn to [*cancelled*] Oceans may become [*substituted*] grey ] P². |
| 19-20. | [*No break*] ] 31, 32. |
| 20. | . . . an [*cancelled*] a doomed [*substituted*] assassin's ] P². |
| 23. | . . . spar ] P², Q². |
| 29. | . . . God is cold [*cancelled*] ] P². |

Q², a copy in Cora Crane's hand, is headed "4."

### 114

The paper on which Draft R² appears suggests that it was prepared before late 1897. See also Appendix III.

| | |
|---|---|
| *Versions* | R², S², 31, 32. |
| Text | |
| 4. | . . . a [*cancelled*] the [*superscribed*] supple-souled ] R². |

S² is a typewritten copy prepared by Cora Crane for inclusion in the edition of Crane's poems described in Katz, "Cora Crane and the Poetry of Stephen Crane."

## 115

| | |
|---|---|
| *Versions* | T², 31, 32. |
| *Text* | |
| 2. | [*Omitted*] ]31, 32. |

## 116

R. W. Stallman, "Stephen Crane: Some New Stories," *Bulletin of the New York Public Library,* LX, 9 (September 1956), 457, dates the notebook in which this poem appears in Crane's New York period of 1893-1894.

| | |
|---|---|
| *Versions* | U², 33. |
| *Text* | [*Title*] A LOST POEM \| By \| STEPHEN CRANE ] 33. |
| 1. | . . . night, ] 33. |
| 1-2. | Flew [*cancelled*] ] U². |
| 4. | . . . eyes, ] 33. |
| 5. | . . . loved, ] 33. |
| 6. | . . . lands [*cancelled*] groves [*substituted*] of ] U². |
| | . . . distance, ] 33. |
| 7. | . . . by [*cancelled*]  at [*superscribed*] the ] U². |
| | . . . sea, ] 33. |
| 8. | . . . leaves. ] 33. |
| 8-9. | And [*cancelled*] ] U². |
| 9. | . . . experience, ] 33. |
| 10. | . . . night. ] 33. |

In the Book Review section of the New York *Herald Tribune* of 22 November 1931, Taylor (the editor of Publication 33) announced the discovery of new material:

> A large packet of unpublished writings by Stephen Crane has been discovered, of the first interest. The material includes notes for MAGGIE, A GIRL OF THE STREETS, THE RED BADGE OF COURAGE, sketches, short stories, poems and dialogues. They are to be published in the spring of 1932. As literary manager of Crane's estate, I should like to communicate with those who have in their possession any Stephen Crane material, letters included.

Evidently, little came of the venture except for the private printing of Publication 33, the reprinting of the poem (with two punctuation variations from Publication 33) in the *Golden Book*, XIX, 110 (February 1934), 189, and the publication of "The Holler Tree" in the same number of the *Golden Book*. (The poem and the story were preceded by a vaunt: "The First Manuscripts by the Author of 'The Red Badge of Courage' to Appear since 1903: A Fable and a Poem from his Unpublished Intimate Notebooks.") While Williams and Starrett, *Stephen Crane: A Bibliography*, p. 71, supply 1932 as the date for the undated Publication 33, a copy in the Columbia University Crane Collection is inscribed "pre-publication copy" and is enclosed in an envelope postmarked 27 February 1933.

## 117

The poem (and the story for which the poem is the epigraph) was probably written in early 1899. See Appendix II.

*Version* 28.

*118*

Linson, *My Stephen Crane,* pp. 13-14, suggests that the
poem was written in December, 1892.

| *Versions* | V², 34. |
|---|---|
| 1. | . . . purs [*cancelled*] haggard ] V². |
| 2. | . . . s [*cancelled*] a ] V². |
| 3. | . . . thee. ] 34. |
| 4. | . . . br [*cancelled*] wan . . . m mann [*cancelled*] ] V². |
| 5. | . . . th [*cancelled*] not ] V². |
| 8, | . . . do [*inserted*] smilest ] V². |
| 9. | . . . reproach me ] 34. |
| 11. | . . . twere ] 34. |
| 16. | . . . riot ] 34. |

Apparently Crane was doodling with words when this poem
was written. (But note that the lament to the empty purse is
in the tradition established as early as Geoffrey Chaucer's *The
Complaint of Chaucer to his Purse.* See also *135.*) The first few
lines of the sheet that contains V² record two false starts: "In a
large vaulted hall that blazed with light. | [two lines of the
sheet are skipped] | I'd sell my steps to the grave at ten cents
per foot, if t'were but honestie."

*119*

Copeland and Day to Crane, 19 October 1894, is evidence
that this poem was written at the time of the composition of
the poems in *The Black Riders.* (See pp. xxvii-xxviii.)

| *Versions* | W², X², 34. |
|---|---|
| *Text* | |
| 3. | . . . gold [*cancelled*] band [*substituted*] he ] W². |

4.      them [*cancelled*] A ] W².

Draft X² is a typescript copy prepared by Cora Crane for her edition of Crane's poems. At the top of the page of this copy, the page number in that edition, "-8-," appears. Draft W² continues with three cancelled lines:

> For shackles fit apes.
> He is not brave
> Who leaves the iron on doves.

Draft X² omits these lines, while 34 prints them in the commentary on the poem.


## 120

This poem was composed at the time of the writing of the poems in *The Black Riders*. See Copeland and Day to Crane, 19 October 1894, pp. xxvii-xxviii.

| | |
|---|---|
| *Versions* | Y², Z², 34. |
| *Text* | |
| 2. | . . . thus, ] 34. |
| 3. | . . . have a glorious apple ] 34. |
| 5. | . . . ancestor ] 34. |
| 8-9. | [*No break*] ] Z², 34. |
| 16. | . . . apple. ] Y², 34. |
| 21-22. | [*No break*] ] Z². |
| 22. | "How then? ] 34. |
| 29. | . . . than god ] Y², Z², 34. |
| 30. | . . . splendour, ] Z². |

Draft Z² is a two page typescript copy prepared by Cora for her edition of Crane's poems. The pages are headed "-6-" and "-7-" but these numbers are cancelled, and "(1)" and "(2)" are substituted. (The first page concludes with line 16.)

*121*

The legal cap fragment on which Draft A³ is written suggests that the date of composition is well before 1897.

| *Versions* | A³, B³, 34. |
| --- | --- |
| *Text* | |
| 2. | . . . it's ] A³. |
| 3. | . . . wilderness, ] B³. |
| 5. | . . . it's ] A³. |
| 6. | . . . low [*cancelled*] wail ] A³. |

Draft B³ is a typescript copy headed "-5-" prepared by Cora for her edition of Crane's poems.

*122*

The legal cap paper of Draft C³ is evidence that the poem was written before 1897. It is possible that this is "The Reformer", reported lost to Hamlin Garland on 9 May 1894 (see Stallman and Gilkes, *Letters,* p. 36 ).

| *Versions* | C³, D³, 34. |
| --- | --- |
| *Text* | |
| 4. | . . . wares ] C³. |
| 6. | . . . wares ] C³, 34. |
| 8. | . . . wares ] C³, 34. |
| 11. | . . . intention [*cancelled*] attention [*superscribed*] of ] C³. . . . intention of] 34. |
| 13. | Help them or hinder them \| As they cry their wares. ] 34. |

Draft D³ is a typescript copy headed "-3-" and prepared by Cora for her edition of Crane's poems.

**123**

The legal cap paper of Draft $E^3$ suggests that the poem was written before 1897. See also Appendix III.

*Versions*  $E^3$, $F^3$, 34.
   *Text*
     2.     . . . the [*cancelled*] a ] $E^3$.
     3.     . . . b [*cancelled*] moon-beams ] $E^3$.
     6.     . . . long [*cancelled*] shadows fal [*cancelled*] adrift [*substituted*] on ] $E^3$.
     9.     . . . canoe ] 34.
     10.    . . . turmoil ] $F^3$.

Draft $F^3$ is a typescript copy headed "-4-" prepared by Cora for her edition of Crane's poems.

**124**

This poem was written during the period from April to May, 1894. See Appendix I.

*Versions*  $G^3$, 34.
   *Text*
     20.    . . . the [*inserted*] breast ] $G^3$.

**125**

Hoffman, *The Poetry of Stephen Crane*, p. 77, suggests that this poem was written in 1895, after Crane's trip to Mexico. Draft $H^3$ was almost certainly typewritten after 1895 (probably in 1899), but the theme and treatment of the poem makes Hoffman's date for the lost manuscript quite reasonable.

*Versions*  $H^3$, 34.

*126*

The analogue contained in the last lines of Crane's letter to Nellie Crouse suggests that the poem was written at about March, 1896.

*Versions*     I³, J³, 34.

In his last letter to Nellie Crouse, an Ohioan whom Crane met in New York in early 1895, Crane acknowledged his defeat in courting her, ending his letter with the traditionary prediction of an unattractive future for himself:

> Dear me, how much am I getting to admire graveyards —the calm unfretting unhopeing end of things—serene absence of passion—oblivious to sin—ignorant of the accursed golden hopes that flame at night and make a man run his legs off and then in the daylight of experience turn out to be ingenious traps for the imagination. If there is a joy of living I cant find it. The future? The future is blue with obligations—new trials —conflicts. It was a rare old wine the gods brewed *for mortals.* Flagons of despair—

The letter is in Stallman and Gilkes, *Letters,* pp. 119-120. See also Cady and Wells, *Stephen Crane's Love Letters to Nellie Crouse.*

Draft J³ is a holograph copy in Cora's hand; the copy is headed "3-".


*127*

This was written in late 1898 or early 1899, after Crane had returned from reporting the Spanish-American War. In all probability, the poem was written after his return to England in February, 1899. This probability stems from the fact that Draft K³ is on a gray-ruled paper that was evidently torn from a notebook of folio size which contained sheets watermarked "CARISBROOK SUPERFINE," and countermarked with the figure of an enthroned Brittania.

| Versions | K³, 34. |
| Text | |
| 11. | . . . Practical [*cancelled*] practical · [*super-scribed*] men, ] K³. |
| 15. | . . . sad sacked city ] 34. . . . home [*cancelled*] record [*substituted*] ] K³. |
| 16. | Furious to face the Spaniard, these people \| And crawling worms before their task ] 34. |

## 128

The poem probably was composed in late 1898.

| Versions | L³, M³, 34. |
| Text | |
| 2. | . . . grinding of ] 34. |
| 3. | . . . villages ] 34. |
| 14. | . . . don't ] 34. |

Draft M³ is a holograph copy, headed "2", in Cora's hand.

## 129

On Draft N³, Cora's typescript and the only surviving copy of the poem, Cora noted that "(The ms., of the above, has just been discovered in saddle-bags used by Stephen Crane during the late war with Spain.) On this basis, it is appropriate to assign 1898 as the year of composition.

| Versions | N³, 34. |
| Text | [*Title*] THE BATTLE HYMN. \| BY. \| STE-PHEN CRANE. ] N³. *The Battle Hymn* ] 34. |

2.        . . . voice of . . . nation: ] 34.
4.        . . . under-light of ] 34.
13+14.    Mark well, mark well, the new path, lead awry ] 34.
17.       . . . thine. ] N³.

Both Gilkes, *Cora Crane,* p. 288, and Hoffman, *The Poetry of Stephen Crane,* p. 158, report that there is one typewritten copy of the poem, and one copy in Cora's hand. A search of the Cranes' papers in the Butler Library of Columbia University reveals only N³ and a carbon copy of N³.

It was Charles Michelson of the New York *Journal* who sent Cora the saddlebags containing the "autograph battle hymn, probably written while your husband was in Cuba." See Michelson to Cora Crane, July 1900, in Gilkes, *Cora Crane,* p. 228n. Michelson had submitted the poem to the *Pall Mall Gazette* where it was rejected. In the Introduction to *Work,* Volume XII, Michelson recalled his association with Crane.

## 130

Crane typed the poem in early 1899, on his own machine.

*Versions*    O³, 34.
8.        . . . shades ] 34.
10-11.    [*No break*] ]34.

## 131

The poem was typed in early 1899, on Crane's typewriter.

*Versions*    P³, 34.
*Text*
9.        . . . pale death-child, ] 34.

12.       . . . manners, ] 34.
15.       . . . silence ] 34.
17.       . . . it's ] P³, 34. . . . pain ] 34.

## 132

*Versions*       Q³, 34.
  *Text*
2.       . . . strains, ] 34.
3.       . . . stinging. ] 34.

## 133

The poem was typewritten by Crane in early 1899.

*Versions*   ,   R³, 34.

## 134

The statement in the poem, and that in the unfinished note on the verso of Draft S³, suggests that this was written towards the end of 1899 or the beginning of 1900. And yet, if the note was written to the editor of the *Westminster Gazette* (the paper which published his Greco-Turkish War articles in May and June, 1897), it might have been a protest against the heavy editing of his articles. In that case, both the note and the poem would derive from about June, 1897. (See, for example, the opening paragraphs of the *Gazette* and the New York *Journal* versions of "Some Interviews," in Stallman and Hagemann, *War Dispatches*, p. 74.) With the evidence available at this point, it is impossible to establish any more definite date of composition of the poem.

*Versions*       S³, 34.
  *Text*
3.       W [*cancelled*] By— ] S³.

The verse is, of course, a parody of Longfellow's "Psalm of Life," which begins

> Tell me not, in mournful numbers,
>   Life is but an empty dream!—
> For the soul is dead that slumbers,
>   And things are not what they seem.

## 135

Drafts T³ and U³ were typewritten in 1899-1900.

*Versions*     T³, U³, 34.
  *Text*
   1.     MY CROSS! ] T³.
   5.     . . . Francs. [*capital* F *cancelled*] ] T³.

While it is apparent that one of the two drafts is a copy of the other, it is impossible to determine with certainty which is the original. The text of U³ is presented in this edition simply because whether line 1 of T³ is a title, or the first line presented in capital letters, neither is characteristic of Crane. Draft T³ probably is a copy by Cora.

*APPENDICES*

## I. GRATITUDE, THE SENSE OF OBLIGATION. . . .

On 9 May 1894, Crane wrote to Hamlin Garland to give him the latest news: he told him that a poem ("The Reformer") that Garland had enjoyed was lost; that Crane had "sat and glowed and shivered" at a performance of Gerhardt Hauptmann's *Hannele* and that he had written "a decoration day thing for the *Press* which aroused them to enthusiasm. They said, in about a minute though, that I was firing over the heads of the soldiers" (Stallman and Gilkes, *Letters*, p. 37). This piece is of unusual interest—despite its weak construction, banal thesis, and sentimental rhetoric—because the first of its six manuscript pages contains "A soldier, young in years, young in ambitions" (*124*), and it is therefore Crane's first attempt at integrating a prose work with a verse epigraph. Daniel G. Hoffman's *The Red Badge of Courage and Other Stories* (New York: Harper and Brothers, 1957), pp. 187-89, first printed the prose work (without the epigraph).

Gratitude, the sense of obligation, often comes very late to the mind of the world. It is the habit of humanity to forget her heroes, her well-doers, until they have passed beyond the sound of earthly voices; then when the loud, praising cries are raised, there comes a regret and a sorrow that those ears are forever deaf to plaudits. It has almost become a great truth that the man who achieves an extraordinary benefit for the race shall go to death without the particular appreciation of his fellows. One by one they go, with no evident knowledge of the value of their services unless their own hearts tell them that in their fidelity to truth and to duty, they have gained a high success.

The men who fought in the great war for freedom and union are disappearing. They are upon their last great march, a march that ceases to be seen at the horizon and whose end is death. We are now viewing the last of the procession, the belated ones, the stragglers. A vast body of them have thronged to the grave, regiment by regiment, brigade by brigade, and the others are hurrying after their fellows who have marched into the Hereafter. There, every company is gradually getting its men, no soldier but what will be there to answer his name, and upon the earth there will remain but a memory of deeds well and stoutly done.

If in the past there is any reflection of the future, we can expect that when the last veteran has vanished there will come a time of great monuments, eulogies, tears. Then the boy in blue will have grown to heroic size, and painters, sculptors, and writers, will have been finally impressed, and strive to royally celebrate the deeds of the brave, simple, quiet men who crowded upon the opposing bayonets of their country's enemies. But no voice penetrates the grave, and the chants and shouts will carry no warmth to dead hearts.

Let us then struggle to defeat this ironical law of fate. Let us not wait to celebrate but consider that there are now before us the belated ones of the army that is marching over the horizon, into the sky, into history and tradition. The laws of the universe sometimes appear to be toying with compensations, holding back results until death closes the eyes to success, bludgeoning   fr of benefactions, rewarding they who do evil. It [is] well that we do all in our power to defeat these things.

Do not then wait. Let not loud and full expression of gratitude come too late to the mind of the nation. Do not forget our heroes, our well-doers, until they have marched to where no little cheers of men can reach them. Remember them now, and if the men of the future forget, the sin is with them. They are ours, these boys in blue, their deeds and their privations, their wondrous patience and endurance, their grim, abiding faith and fortitude are ours. Let us expend our lungs then while they can hear; let us throw up our caps while they can see, these veterans whose feet are still sore from marches, in whose old grey hairs the pages and paragraphs of future histories are nothing. Our obligation exists in the present, and it is fit that we leave not too much to future historians.

Upon this day, those who are left go sadly, a little pitiable handful, to decorate the places of their comrades' rest. When the small solemn flower-ladened processions start for the graves, it

232

is well to be with them. There are to be learned there lessons of patriotism that are good for us at this day. No harm would come if we allowed the stores to have less rush and crowd. We cannot afford to neglect the spectacle of our bearded, bronzed and wrinkled men in blue tramping slowly and haltingly to bestow their gifts upon sleeping places of those who are gone. And it is well then to think of the time when these men were in the flush of vigor and manhood and went with the firm-swinging steps of youth to do their duty to their God, their homes and their country.

When they are gone, American society has lost its most valuable element for they have paid the price of patriotism, they know the meaning of patriotism, and stars shot from guns would not hinder their devotion to the flag which they rescued from dust and oblivion. Let us watch with apprehension this departure of an army, one by one, one by one. Let the last words that they hear from us be words of gratitude and affection.

It is just and proper that we go with them to the graves, that they may see that when they too are gone, there will be many to come to their graves, that their camping grounds and battle fields will be remembered places and that the lesson of their lives will be taught to children who will never see their faces.

Great are the nation's dead who sleep in peace. May all old comrades gather at an eternal camp-fire. May the sweet, wind-waved rustle of trees be over them, may the long, lush grass and flowers be about their feet. Peace and rest be with them forever, for they have done well.

## II. THE CLAN OF NO-NAME

Early in 1899, as Frederick A. Stokes was preparing to issue *War Is Kind*, Crane made a second attempt at preceding a prose work with a verse epigraph. If the first attempt saw him "firing over the heads of the soldiers," "The Clan of No-Name" is a reasonably successful integration of epigraph and tale. The envelope structure of the poem (*117*) is paralleled by the structure of the story; the significance of the birds circling the mutilated body of Manolo is given greater effect by the coupling of hawks and time in the epigraph; and the betrayal by death and by the falsity of the love affair are linked within the preceding seven lines. The weakest note in the epigraph is the introduction of the personal symbol of drowning, and yet even this heightens the sense of the irony of life as both the poem and the tale reflect on the central line of the poem. The story is reprinted from *Wounds in the Rain* (New York: Frederick A. Stokes Company, 1900), pp. 42-73.

### I

She was out in the garden. Her mother came to her rapidly. "Margharita! Margharita, Mister Smith is here! Come!" Her mother was fat and commercially excited. Mister Smith was a matter of some importance to all Tampa people, and since he was really in love with Margharita he was distinctly of more importance to this particular household.

Palm trees tossed their sprays over the fence toward the rutted sand of the street. A little foolish fishpond in the center of the garden emitted a sound of redfins flipping, flipping. "No, mamma," said the girl; "let Mr. Smith wait. I like the garden in the moonlight."

Her mother threw herself into that state of virtuous astonishment which is the weapon of her kind. "Margharita!"

The girl evidently considered herself to be a privileged belle, for she answered quite carelessly, "Oh, let him wait."

The mother threw abroad her arms with a semblance of great high-minded suffering and withdrew. Margharita walked alone in the moonlit garden. Also an electric light threw its shivering gleam over part of her parade.

There was peace for a time. Then, suddenly, through the faint brown palings was stuck an envelope white and square. Margharita approached this envelope with an indifferent stride. She hummed a silly air, she bore herself casually, but there was something that made her grasp it hard, a peculiar muscular exhibition, not discernible to indifferent eyes. She did not clutch it, but she took it—simply took it in a way that meant everything, and, to measure it by vision, it was a picture of the most complete disregard.

She stood straight for a moment; then she drew from her bosom a photograph and thrust it through the palings. She walked rapidly into the house.

## II

A man in garb of blue and white—something related to what we call bed-ticking—was seated in a curious little cupola on the top of a Spanish blockhouse. The blockhouse sided a white military road that curved away from the man's sight into a blur of trees. On all sides of him were fields of tall grass, studded with palms and lined with fences of barbed wire. The sun beat aslant through the trees, and the man sped his eyes deep into the dark tropical shadows, that seemed velvet with coolness. These tranquil vistas resembled painted scenery in a theater, and, moreover, a hot, heavy silence lay upon the land.

The soldier in the watching place leaned an unclean Mauser rifle in a corner and, reaching down, took a glowing coal on a bit of palm bark handed up to him by a comrade. The men below were mainly asleep. The sergeant in command drowsed near the open door, the arm above his head showing his long keen-angled chevrons, attached carelessly with safety pins. The sentry lit his cigarette and puffed languorously.

Suddenly he heard from the air around him the querulous, deadly swift spit of rifle bullets; and an instant later the poppety-pop of a small volley sounded in his face, close, as if it were fired only ten feet away. Involuntarily he threw back his head quickly, as if he were protecting his nose from a falling tile. He screamed an alarm and fell into the blockhouse. In the gloom of it, men with their breaths coming sharply between their teeth were tumbling wildly for positions at the loopholes. The door had been slammed, but the sergeant lay just within, propped up as when he drowsed, but now with blood flowing steadily over the hand that he pressed flatly to his chest. His face was in stark yellow agony; he chokingly repeated: "Fuego! Por Dios, hombres!"

The men's ill-conditioned weapons were jammed through the loopholes, and they began to fire from all four sides of the blockhouse, from the simple datum, apparently, that the enemy were in the vicinity. The fumes of burnt powder grew stronger and stronger in the little square fortress. The rattling of the magazine locks was incessant, and the interior might have been that of a gloomy manufactory if it were not for the sergeant down under the feet of the men, coughing out: "Por Dios, hombres! Por Dios! Fuego!"

## III

A string of five Cubans, in linen that had turned earthy brown in color, slid through the woods at a pace that was neither a walk nor a run. It was a kind of rack. In fact, the whole manner of the men, as they thus moved, bore a rather comic resemblance to the American pacing horse. But they had come many miles since sunup over mountainous and half-marked paths, and were plainly still fresh. The men were all practicos—guides. They made no sound in their swift travel, but moved their half-shod feet with the skill of cats. The woods lay around them in a deep silence, such as one might find at the bottom of a lake.

Suddenly the leading practico raised his hand. The others pulled up short and dropped the butts of their weapons calmly and noiselessly to the ground. The leader whistled a low note, and immediately another practico appeared from the bushes. He moved close to the leader without a word, and then they spoke in whispers.

"There are twenty men and a sergeant in the blockhouse."

"And the road?":

"One company of cavalry passed to the east this morning at seven o'clock. They were escorting four carts. An hour later, one horseman rode swiftly to the westward. About noon, ten infantry soldiers with a corporal were taken from the big fort and put in the first blockhouse to the east of the fort. There were already twelve men there. We saw a Spanish column moving off toward Mariel.

"No more?"

"No more."

"Good. But the cavalry?"

"It is all right. They were going a long march."

"The expedition is a half league behind. Go and tell the general."

The scout disappeared. The five other men lifted their guns and resumed their rapid and noiseless progress. A moment later no sound broke the stillness save the thump of a mango, as it dropped lazily from its tree to the grass. So strange had been the apparition of these men, their dress had been so allied in color to the soil, their passing had so little disturbed the solemn rumination of the forest, and their going had been so like a spectral dissolution, that a witness could have wondered if he dreamed.

IV

A small expedition had landed with arms from the United States, and had now come out of the hills and to the edge of a wood. Before them was a long-grassed rolling prairie marked with palms. A half mile away was the military road, and they could see the top of a blockhouse. The insurgent scouts were moving somewhere off in the grass. The general sat comfortably under a tree, while his staff of three young officers stood about him chatting. Their linen clothing was notable from being distinctly whiter than that of the men who, one hundred and fifty in number, lay on the ground in a long brown fringe, ragged—indeed, bare in many places—but singularly reposeful, unworried, veteran-like.

The general, however, was thoughtful. He pulled continually at his little thin mustache. As far as the heavily patrolled and guarded military road was concerned, the insurgents had been in the habit of dashing across it in small bodies whenever they pleased, but to safely scoot over it with a valuable convoy of arms was decidedly a more important thing. So the general awaited the return of his practicos with anxiety. The still pampas betrayed no sign of their existence.

The general gave some orders, and an officer counted off twenty men to go with him and delay any attempt of the troop of calvary to return from the eastward. It was not an easy task, but it was a familiar task—checking the advance of a greatly superior force by a very hard fire from concealment. A few rifles had often bayed a strong column for sufficient length of time for all strategic purposes. The twenty men pulled themselves together tranquilly. They looked quite indifferent. Indeed, they had the supremely casual manner of old soldiers, hardened to battle as a condition of existence.

Thirty men were then told off, whose function it was to worry and rag at the blockhouse and check any advance from the westward. A hundred men, carrying precious burdens—besides their own equipment—were to pass in as much of a rush as possible between these two wings, cross the road, and skip for the hills, their retreat being covered by a combination of the two firing parties. It was a trick that needed both luck and neat arrangement. Spanish columns were for ever prowling through this province in all directions and at all times. Insurgent bands—the lightest of light infantry—were kept on the jump, even when they were not incommoded by fifty boxes, each one large enough for the coffin of a little man, and heavier than if the little man were in it, and fifty small but formidable boxes of ammunition.

The carriers stood to their boxes, and the firing parties leaned on their rifles. The general arose and strolled to and fro, his hands behind him. Two of his staff were jesting at the third, a young man with a face less bronzed, and with very new accoutrements. On the strap of his cartouche were a gold star and a silver star, placed in a horizontal line, denoting that he was a second lieutenant. He seemed very happy; he laughed at all their jests, although his eye roved continually over the sunny grasslands, where was going to happen his first fight. One of his stars was bright, like his hopes; the other was pale, like death.

Two practicos came racking out of the grass. They spoke rapidly to the general; he turned and nodded to his officers. The two firing parties filed out and diverged toward their positions.

The general watched them through his glasses. It was strange to note how soon they were dim to the unaided eye. The little patches of brown in the green grass did not look like men at all.

Practicos continually ambled up to the general. Finally he turned and made a sign to the bearers. The first twenty men in line picked up their boxes, and this movement rapidly spread to the tail of the line. The weighted procession moved painfully out upon the sunny prairie. The general, marching at the head of it, glanced continually back, as if he were compelled to drag behind him some ponderous iron chain. Besides the obvious mental worry, his face bore an expression of intense physical strain, and he even bent his shoulders, unconsciously tugging at the chain to hurry it through this enemy-crowded valley.

## V

The fight was opened by eight men who, snuggling in the grass within three hundred yards of the blockhouse, suddenly blazed away at the bed-ticking figure in the cupola and at the open door, where they could see vague outlines. Then they laughed and yelled insulting language, for they knew that, as far as the Spaniards were concerned, the surprise was as much as having a diamond bracelet turn to soap. It was this volley that smote the sergeant and caused the man in the cupola to scream and tumble from his perch.

The eight men, as well as all other insurgents within fair range, had chosen good positions for lying close, and for a time they let the blockhouse rage, although the soldiers therein could occasionally hear, above the clamor of their weapons shrill and almost wolfish calls coming from men whose lips were laid against the ground. But it is not in the nature of them of Spanish blood, and armed with rifles, to long endure the sight of anything so tangible as an enemy's blockhouse without shooting at it—other conditions being partly favorable. Presently the steaming soldiers in the little fort could hear the sping and shiver of bullets striking the wood that guarded their bodies.

A perfectly white smoke floated up over each firing Cuban, the penalty of the Remington rifle, but about the blockhouse there was only the lightest gossamer of blue. The blockhouse stood always for some big, clumsy, and rather incompetent animal, while the insurgents, scattered on two sides of it, were little enterprising creatures of another species, too wise to come too near, but joyously raging at its easiest flanks and dirling the lead into its sides in a way to make it fume and spit and rave like the tom-cat when the glad free-band foxhound pups catch him in the lane.

The men, outlying in the grass, chuckled deliriously at the fury of the Spanish fire. They howled opprobrium to encourage the Spaniards to fire more ill-used, incapable bullets. Whenever an insurgent was about to fire, he ordinarily prefixed the affair with a speech. "Do you want something to eat? Yes? All right." Bang! "Eat that." The more common expressions of the incredibly foul Spanish tongue were trifles light as air in this badinage, which was shrieked out from the grass during the spin of bullets and the dull rattle of the shooting.

But at some time there came a series of sounds from the east, that began in a few disconnected pruts and ended as if an amateur was trying to play the long roll upon a muffled drum. Those of the insurgents in the blockhouse-attacking party who had neighbors in the grass turned and looked at them seriously. They knew what the new sound meant. It meant that the twenty men who had gone to the eastward were now engaged. A column of some kind was approaching from that direction, and they knew by the chatter that it was a solemn occasion.

In the first place, they were now on the wrong side of the road. They were obliged to cross it to rejoin the main body, provided, of course, that the main body succeeded itself in crossing it. To accomplish this, the party at the blockhouse would have to move to the eastward until out of sight or good range of the maddened little fort. But, judging from the heaviness of the firing, the party of twenty who protected the east were almost sure to be driven immediately back. Hence travel in that direction would become exceedingly hazardous. Hence a man looked seriously at his neighbor. It might easily be that in a moment they were to become an isolated force and woefully on the wrong side of the road.

Any retreat to the westward was absurd, since primarily they would have to widely circle the blockhouse, and, more than that,

they could hear even now, in that direction, Spanish bugle calling
to Spanish bugle far and near, until one would think that every
man in Cuba was a trumpeter and had come forth to parade his
talent.

## VI

The insurgent general stood in the middle of the road gnawing
his lips. Occasionally, he stamped a foot and beat his hands pas-
sionately together. The carriers were streaming past him, patient,
sweating fellows, bowed under their burdens, but they could not
move fast enough for him when others of his men were engaged
both to the east and to the west, and he, too, knew from the sound
that those to the east were in a sore way. Moreover, he could hear
that accursed bugling, bugling, bugling, in the west.

He turned suddenly to the new lieutenant, who stood behind
him, pale and quiet. "Did you ever think a hundred men were so
many?" he cried, incensed to the point of beating them. Then he
said longingly: "Oh, for a half an hour! Or even twenty min-
utes!"

A practico racked violently up from the east. It is characteristic
of these men that, although they take a certain roadster gait and
hold it for ever, they cannot really run, sprint, race. "Captain
Rodriguez is attacked by two hundred men, señor, and the cavalry
is behind them. He wishes to know—"

The general was furious; he pointed. "Go! Tell Rodriguez to
hold his place for twenty minutes, even if he leaves every man
dead."

The practico shambled hastily off.

The last of the carriers were swarming across the road. The
rifle-drumming in the east was swelling out and out, evidently
coming slowly nearer. The general bit his nails. He wheeled
suddenly upon the young lieutenant. "Go to Bas at the block-
house. Tell him to hold the devil himself for ten minutes and
then bring his men out of that place."

The long line of bearers was crawling like a dun worm toward
the safety of the foothills. High bullets sang a faint song over the
aide as he saluted. The bugles had in the west ceased, and that
was more ominous than bugling. It meant that the Spanish troops
were about to march, or perhaps that they had marched.

The young lieutenant ran along the road until he came to the bend which marked the range of sight from the blockhouse. He drew his machete, his stunning new machete, and hacked feverishly at the barbed wire fence which lined the north side of the road at that point. The first wire was obdurate, because it was too high for his stroke, but two more cut like candy, and he stepped over the remaining one, tearing his trousers in passing on the lively serpentine ends of the severed wires. Once out in the field, and bullets seemed to know him and call for him and speak their wish to kill him. But he ran on, because it was his duty, and because he would be shamed before men if he did not do his duty, and because he was desolate out there all alone in the fields with death.

A man running in this manner from the rear was in immensely greater danger than those who lay snug and close. But he did not know it. He thought, because he was five hundred—four hundred and fifty—four hundred yards away from the enemy and the others were only three hundred yards away, that they were in far more peril. He ran to join them because of his opinion. He did not care to do it, but he thought that was what men of his kind would do in such a case. There was a standard, and he must follow it, obey it, because it was a monarch, the Prince of Conduct.

A bewildered and alarmed face raised itself from the grass, and a voice cried to him: "Drop, Manolo! Drop! Drop!" He recognized Bas and flung himself to the earth beside him.

"Why," he said panting, "what's the matter?"

"Matter?" said Bas. "You are one of the most desperate and careless officers I know. When I saw you coming I wouldn't have given a peseta for your life."

"Oh, no," said the young aide. Then he repeated his orders rapidly. But he was hugely delighted. He knew Bas well; Bas was a pupil of Maceo; Bas invariably led his men; he never was a mere spectator of their battle; he was known for it throughout the western end of the island. The new officer had early achieved a part of his ambition—to be called a brave man by established brave men.

"Well, if we get away from her quickly it will be better for us," said Bas, bitterly. "I've lost six men killed, and more wounded. Rodriguez can't hold his position there, and in a little time more than a thousand men will come from the other direction."

He hissed a low call, and later the young aide saw some of the men sneaking off with the wounded, lugging them on their backs as porters carry sacks. The fire from the blockhouse had become aweary, and as the insurgent fire also slackened, Bas and the young lieutenant lay in the weeds listening to the approach of the eastern fight, which was sliding toward them like a door to shut them off.

Bas groaned. "I leave my dead. Look there." He swung his hand in a gesture, and the lieutenant, looking, saw a corpse. He was not stricken as he expected; there was very little blood; it was a mere thing.

"Time to travel," said Bas suddenly. His imperative hissing brought his men near him; there were a few hurried questions and answers; then, characteristically, the men turned in the grass, lifted their rifles, and fired a last volley into the blockhouse, accompanying it with their shrill cries. Scrambling low to the ground, they were off in a winding line for safety. Breathing hard, the lieutenant stumbled his way forward. Behind him he could hear the men calling each to each: "Segue! Segue! Segue! Go on! Get out! Git!" Everybody understood that the peril of crossing the road was compounding from minute to minute.

## VII

When they reached the gap through which the expedition had passed, they fled out upon the road like scared wild fowl tracking along a sea-beach. A cloud of blue figures far up this dignified shaded avenue fired at once. The men already had begun to laugh as they shied one by one across the road. "Segue! Segue!" The hard part for the nerves had been the lack of information of the amount of danger. Now that they could see it, they accounted it all the more lightly for their previous anxiety.

Over in the other field, Bas and the young lieutenant found Rodriguez, his machete in one hand, his revolver in the other, smoky, dirty, sweating. He shrugged his shoulders when he saw them and pointed disconsolately to the brown thread of carriers moving toward the foothills. His own men were crouched in line just in front of him, blazing like a prairie fire.

Now began the fight of a scant rear guard to hold back the pressing Spaniards until the carriers could reach the top of the ridge, a mile away. This ridge, by the way, was more steep than any roof; it conformed more to the sides of a French warship. Trees grew vertically from it, however, and a man burdened only with his rifle usually pulled himself wheezingly up in a sort of ladder-climbing process, grabbing the slim trunks above him. How the loaded carriers were to conquer it in a hurry, no one knew. Rodriguez shrugged his shoulders as one who would say with philosophy, smiles, tears, courage: "Isn't this a mess!"

At an order, the men scattered back for four hundred yards with the rapidity and mystery of a handful of pebbles flung in the night. They left one behind who cried out, but it was now a game in which some were sure to be left behind to cry out.

The Spaniards deployed on the road and for twenty minutes remained there, pouring into the field such a fire from their magazines as was hardly heard at Gettysburg. As a matter of truth the insurgents were at this time doing very little shooting, being chary of ammunition. But it is possible for the soldier to confuse himself with his own noise, and undoubtedly the Spanish troops thought throughout their din that they were being fiercely engaged. Moreover, a firing line—particularly at night or when opposed to a hidden foe—is nothing less than an emotional chord, a chord of a harp that sings because a puff of air arrives or when a bit of down touches it. This is always true of new troops or stupid troops, and these troops were rather stupid troops. But the way in which they mowed the verdure in the distance was a sight for a farmer.

Presently the insurgents slunk back to another position, where they fired enough shots to stir again the Spaniards into an opinion that they were in a heavy fight. But such a misconception could only endure for a number of minutes. Presently it was plain that the Spaniards were about to advance, and, moreover, word was brought to Rodriguez that a small band of guerillas were already making an attempt to worm around the right flank. Rodriguez cursed despairingly; he sent both Bas and the young

245

lieutenant to that end of the line to hold the men to their work as long as possible.

In reality the men barely needed the presence of their officers. The kind of fighting left practically everything to the discretion of the individual, and they arrived at concert of action mainly because of the equality of experience in the wisdoms of bush-whacking.

The yells of the guerillas could plainly be heard, and the insurgents answered in kind. The young lieutenant found desperate work on the right flank. The men were raving mad with it, babbling, tearful, almost frothing at the mouth. Two terrible bloody creatures passed him, creeping on all fours, and one in a whimper was calling upon God, his mother, and a saint. The guerillas, as effectually concealed as the insurgents, were driving their bullets low through the smoke at sight of a flame, a movement of the grass, or sight of a patch of dirty brown coat. They were no column-o'-four soldiers; they were as slinky and snaky and quick as so many Indians. They were, moreover, native Cubans, and because of their treachery to the one-star flag they never by any chance received quarter if they fell into the hands of the insurgents. Nor, if the case was reversed, did they ever give quarter. It was life and life, death and death; there was no middle ground, no compromise. If a man's crowd was rapidly retreating and he was tumbled over by a slight hit, he should curse the sacred graves that the wound was not through the precise center of his heart. The machete is a fine broad blade, but it is not so nice as a drilled hole in the chest; no man wants his deathbed to be a shambles. The men fighting on the insurgents' right knew that if they fell they were lost.

On the extreme right, the young lieutenant found five men in a little saucer-like hollow. Two were dead, one was wounded and staring blankly at the sky, and two were emptying hot rifles furiously. Some of the guerillas had snaked into positions only a hundred yards away.

The young man rolled in among the men in the saucer. He could hear the barking of the guerillas and the screams of the two insurgents. The rifles were popping and spitting in his face, it seemed, while the whole land was alive with a noise of rolling and drumming. Men could have gone drunken in all this flashing and flying and snarling and din, but at this time he was very deliberate. He knew that he was thrusting himself into a trap whose door, once closed, opened only when the black hand knocked; and every part of him seemed to be in panic-stricken revolt. But something controlled him; something moved him inexorably in one direction; he perfectly understood, but he was only sad, sad with a serene dignity, with the countenance of a mournful young prince. He was of a kind—that seemed to be it; and the men of his kind, on peak or plain, from the dark northern ice fields to the hot wet jungles, through all wine and want, through all lies and unfamiliar truth, dark or light—the men of his kind were governed by their gods, and each man knew the law and yet could not give tongue to it, but it was the law; and if the spirits of the men of his kind were all sitting in critical judgment upon him even then in the sky, he could not have bettered his conduct; he needs must obey the law, and always with the law there is only one way. But from peak and plain, from dark northern ice fields and hot wet jungles, through wine and want, through all lies and unfamiliar truth, dark or light, he heard breathed to him the approval and the benediction of his brethren.

He stooped and gently took a dead man's rifle and some cartridges. The battle was hurrying, hurrying, hurrying, but he was in no haste. His glance caught the staring eye of the wounded soldier, and he smiled at him quietly. The man—simple doomed peasant—was not of his kind, but the law on fidelity was clear.

He thrust a cartridge into the Remington and crept up beside the two unhurt men. Even as he did so, three or four bullets cut so close to him that all his flesh tingled. He fired carefully into the smoke. The guerillas were certainly not now more than fifty yards away.

He raised him coolly for his second shot, and almost instantly it was as if some giant had struck him in the chest with a beam. It whirled him in a great spasm back into the saucer. As he put his two hands to his breast, he could hear the guerillas screeching exultantly, every throat vomiting forth all the infamy of a language prolific in the phrasing of infamy.

One of the other men came rolling slowly down the slope,

while his rifle followed him and, striking another rifle, clanged out. Almost immediately the survivor howled and fled wildly. A whole volley missed him, and then one or more shots caught him as a bird is caught on the wing.

The young lieutenant's body seemed galvanized from head to foot. He concluded that he was not hurt very badly, but when he tried to move he found that he could not lift his hands from his breast. He had turned to lead. He had had a plan of taking a photograph from his pocket and looking at it.

There was a stir in the grass at the edge of the saucer, and a man appeared there, looking where lay the four insurgents. His negro face was not an eminently ferocious one in its lines, but now it was lit with an illimitable blood-greed. He and the young lieutenant exchanged a singular glance; then he came stepping eagerly down. The young lieutenant closed his eyes, for he did not want to see the flash of the machete.

## VIII

The Spanish colonel was in a rage, and yet immensely proud; immensely proud, and yet in a rage of disappointment. There had been a fight, and the insurgents had retreated, leaving their dead; but still a valuable expedition had broken through his lines and escaped to the mountains. As a matter of truth, he was not sure whether to be wholly delighted or wholly angry, for well he knew that the importance lay not so much in the truthful account of the action as it did in the heroic prose of the official report, and in the fight itself lay material for a purple splendid poem. The insurgents had run away; no one could deny it; it was plain even to whatever privates had fired with their eyes shut. This was worth a loud blow and splutter. However, when all was said and done, he could not help but reflect that if he had captured this expedition he would have been a brigadier general, if not more.

He was a short, heavy man with a beard, who walked in a manner common to all elderly Spanish officers, and to many young ones; that is to say, he walked as if his spine was a stick and a little longer than his body; as if he suffered from some disease of the backbone which allowed him but scant use of his

248

legs. He toddled along the road, gesticulating disdainfully and muttering: "Ca! Ca! Ca!"

He berated some soldiers for an immaterial thing, and as he approached, the men stepped precipitately back, as if he were a fire engine. They were most of them young fellows who displayed, when under orders, the manner of so many faithful dogs. At present they were black, tongue-hanging, thirsty boys, bathed in the nervous weariness of the after-battle time.

Whatever he may truly have been in character, the colonel closely resembled a gluttonous and libidinous old pig, filled from head to foot with the pollution of a sinful life. "Ca!" he snarled, as he toddled. "Ca! Ca!" The soldiers saluted as they backed to the side of the road. The air was full of the odor of burnt rags. Over on the prairie guerillas and regulars were rummaging the grass. A few unimportant shots sounded from near the base of the hills.

A guerilla, glad with plunder, came to a Spanish captain. He held in his hand a photograph. "Mira, señor. I took this from the body of an officer whom I killed machete to machete."

The captain shot from the corner of his eye a cynical glance at the guerilla, a glance which commented upon the last part of the statement. "M-m-m," he said. He took the photograph and gazed with a slow faint smile, the smile of a man who knows bloodshed and homes and love, at the face of a girl. He turned the photograph presently, and on the back of it was written: "One lesson in English I will give you—this: I love you. Margharita." The photograph had been taken in Tampa.

The officer was silent for a half minute, while his face still wore the slow faint smile. "Pobrecito," he murmured finally, with a philosophic sigh which was brother to a shrug. Without deigning a word to the guerilla he thrust the photograph in his pocket and walked away.

High over the green earth, in the dizzy blue heights, some great birds were slowly circling with down-turned beaks.

## IX

Margharita was in the gardens. The blue electric rays shone

through the plumes of the palm and shivered in feathery images on the walk. In the little foolish fishpond some stalwart fish was apparently bullying the others, for often there sounded a frantic splashing.

Her mother came to her rapidly. "Margharita! Mister Smith is here! Come!"

"Oh, is he?" cried the girl. She followed her mother to the house. She swept into the little parlor with a grand air, the egotism of a savage. Smith had heard the whirl of her skirts in the hall, and his heart, as usual, thumped hard enough to make him gasp. Every time he called, he would sit waiting with the dull fear in his breast that her mother would enter and indifferently announce that she had gone up to heaven or off to New York with one of his dream rivals, and he would never see her again in this wide world. And he would conjure up tricks to then escape from the house without any one observing his face break up into furrows. It was part of his love to believe in the absolute treachery of his adored one. So whenever he heard the whirl of her skirts in the hall he felt that he had again leased happiness from a dark fate.

She was rosily beaming and all in white. "Why, Mister Smith," she exclaimed, as if he was the last man in the world she expected to see.

"Good-evenin'," he said, shaking hands nervously. He was always awkward and unlike himself at the beginning of one of these calls. It took him some time to get into form.

She posed her figure in operatic style on a chair before him, and immediately galloped off a mile of questions, information of herself, gossip and general outcries which left him no obligation but to look beamingly intelligent and from time to time say "Yes?" His personal joy, however, was to stare at her beauty.

When she stopped and wandered as if uncertain which way to talk, there was a minute of silence, which each of them had been educated to feel was very incorrect; very incorrect indeed. Polite people always babbled at each other like two brooks.

He knew that the responsibility was upon him, and, although his mind was mainly upon the form of the proposal of marriage which he intended to make later, it was necessary that he should

maintain his reputation as a well-bred man by saying something
at once. I flashed upon him to ask: "Won't you please play?"
But the time for the piano ruse was not yet; it was too early. So
he said the first thing that came into his head: "Too bad about
young Manolo Prat being killed over there in Cuba, wasn't it?"

"Wasn't it a pity?" she answered.

"They say his mother is heartbroken," he continued. "They're
afraid she's goin' to die."

"And wasn't it queer that we didn't hear about it for almost
two months?"

"Well, it's no use tryin' to git quick news from there."

Presently they advanced to matters more personal, and she
used upon him a series of star-like glances which crumpled him
at once to squalid slavery. He gloated upon her, afraid, afraid, yet
more avaricious than a thousand misers. She fully comprehended;
she laughed and taunted him with her eyes. She impressed upon
him that she was like a will-'o-the-wisp, beautiful beyond compare,
but impossible, almost impossible, at least very difficult; then
again, suddenly, impossible—impossible—impossible. He was glum;
he would never dare propose to this radiance; it was like asking
to be pope.

A moment later, there chimed into the room something that he
knew to be a more tender note. The girl became dreamy as she
looked at him; her voice lowered to a delicious intimacy of tone.
He leaned forward; he was about to outpour his bully-ragged
soul in fine words, when—presto—she was the most casual person
he had ever laid eyes upon, and was asking him about the route
of the proposed trolley line.

But nothing short of a fire could stop him now. He grabbed her
hand. "Margharita," he murmured gutturally, "I want you to
marry me."

She glared at him in the most perfect lie of astonishment.
"What do you say?"

He arose, and she thereupon arose also and fled back a step.
He could only stammer out her name. And thus they stood, defy-
ing the principles of the dramatic art.

"I love you," he said at last.

"How—how do I know you really—truly love me?" she said,

raising her eyes timorously to his face; and this timorous glance, this one timorous glance, made him the superior person in an instant. He went forward as confident as a grenadier, and, taking both her hands, kissed her.

That night she took a stained photograph from her dressing table and, holding it over the candle, burned it to nothing, her red lips meanwhile parted with the intentness of her occupation. On the back of the photograph was written: "One lesson in English I will give you—this: I love you."

For the word is clear only to the kind who on peak or plain, from dark northern ice fields to the hot wet jungles, through all wine and want, through lies and unfamiliar truth, dark or light, are governed by the unknown gods; and, though each man knows the law, no man may give tongue to it.

# III. TWO LISTS

On a sheet of yellow wove paper, 6 11/16 x 9 14/16 inches, Crane made a list of poems and the periodicals in which they appeared. While there are fifteen numbers in the left-hand margin of the sheet, only the first twelve numbers were used:

| | | | | |
|---|---|---|---|---|
| [101] | 1 | The Lantern Song | Philistine | [4] |
| [82] | 2 | The White Birches | Philistine | [5] |
| [94] | 3 | The Death-demon | Philistine | [3] |
| [78] | 4 | The Sea—Point of View | Philistine | [12] |
| [83] | 5 | The Knight and His Horse | Philistine | [13] |
| [77] | 6 | The Sea to the Pines | Philistine | [13] |
| [76] | 7 | The Drums of the Regiment | Bookman | [6] |
| [89] | 8 | The City | Philistine | [6] |
| [93] | 9 | The Prayer of the Mountains | Chap-book | [11] |
| [84] | 10 | The Candid Man | . . . . . | [24] |
| [74] | 11 | The Call [*cancelled*] Blue Battalions | | [21] |
| [113] | 12 | The [*cancelled*] "A man afloat on a slim spar | | [31] |

The numbers in brackets are supplied: those on the left are the poems to which Crane's titles probably apply, while those on the right are the numbers of the first publication of the poems. The earliest publication of a poem on the list is that of *94* (Crane's number 3) which was published in August, 1895; the latest poem for which acceptance is noted is *83* (Crane's number 5) which was published in May, 1896. Therefore, the list was composed between May, 1896, and June, 1898, the date of publication of *74* (Crane's number 11). (See also Hoffman, *The Poetry of Stephen Crane,* pp. 94, 163.)

At about the same time that the list of magazine acceptances was compiled, Crane made another list of poems. The function of this list, on the legal cap paper that he used for many of his manuscripts, is obscure. It contains the titles of twelve poems, but while the first eight titles appear in the sequence of published poems on the first list, the duplication ends there:

The Shell and the Pines
War is kind
The Prayer of the Peaks
The Candid Man
The Knight rode fast—
The Lantern Song
Chatter of a Death-Demon in a tree top
The Noise of the City
=　　　=　　　=
Chant you loud of punishments
I explain the path of a ship
If you would seek a friend
Oh night dismal, night glorious

254

# Index of First Lines

## Index of First Lines

# DATE DUE

| | | | |
|---|---|---|---|
| | | | |
| | | | |
| | | | |
| | | | |
| | | | |
| | | | |
| | | | |
| | | | |
| | | | |
| | | | |
| | | | |
| | | | |
| | | | |
| | | | |
| | | | |
| | | | |
| | | | |
| | | | |
| | | | PRINTED IN U.S.A. |